words to eat by

words to eat by

using the power of self-talk
to transform your relationship
with food and your body

KAREN R. KOENIG, LCSW, ME.D.

TURNER PUBLISHING COMPANY

Turner Publishing Company
Nashville, Tennessee
www.turnerpublishing.com

Book design: Tim Holtz

Library of Congress Cataloging-in-Publication Data Upon Request

9781684425082   Paperback
9781684425952   Hardback
9781684425105   Ebook

Printed in the United States of America
17 18 19 20 10 9 8 7 6 5 4 3 2

To my clients who keep me on my toes:
I hope I give to you as much as you give to me.

CONTENTS

ACKNOWLEDGMENTS

My heartfelt thanks go to the people who read early drafts of the book and helped shape it into its final form by giving me supportive, honest feedback: Paige O'Mahoney, MD, CHWC of Deliberate Life Wellness; Mary Anne Cohen, LCSW, BCD, director of the New York Center for Eating Disorders; Cathy G. Duke, LPC; and Marian L. Tillotson, Ph.D. As well, I appreciate all the encouragement and expertise, artistic and editorial, provided by Turner Publishing. And, as always, gratitude to my husband, who cheerleads me from book to book in his own quiet way.

INTRODUCTION

When I was a young girl—an only child (or as I joked to myself, a lonely only)—I had an imaginary friend named Jane. She was the voice in my head that acted as a guide to what was best for me in the big, wide world. Why dub her Jane? I haven't the foggiest. But Jane spoke to me as if she were a real person, not simply an imaginary character I'd invented. With an unwavering and unerring sense of what was right and wrong, soothing compassion for my ignorance and foibles, and infinite patience with my questions, she seemed to feel it was her duty to ensure that I lead the best life possible, which meant mentoring me along the way every minute of every day.

To set the record straight, in no sense did I view Jane as a companion or playmate with whom to hang out. I did have two imaginary friends who often accompanied me when I was out and about, but that's another story. Jane was the wise and sometimes-wiseass voice I could depend on to set me straight when I needed to be set straight because she possessed the worldly knowledge I lacked. She was the best mother, father, sister, brother, teacher, friend, mentor, and guardian that anyone could ever have, my inner therapist long before I had any idea what a therapist was. She was simply there when I needed her, no questions asked, and always offered me the best advice to be had at whatever age I was or whatever situation I was in.

Jane's voice could be hypnotic, as when she'd singsong, "Let's not do that. Let's not do that." She knew when she could chide me a bit and say things like, "Oh, c'mon, you don't really believe that, do you? You know better." Alternately, there were times when she sounded a bit like a scared child herself and would whisper, "Let's go, something's not right," with such insistence that I wouldn't dare argue with her. Countless times during my adolescence when my parents caught me doing things I wasn't supposed to be doing, rather than try to suppress a giggle, she'd say something like, "Uh oh, now you've done it. You're in big trouble, missy."

Somewhere along the way, Jane's calming, steady, and sooth-ing voice came to me less and less. My own thoughts matured and evolved as my sense of self blossomed. As my thinking became less muddled and more rational, Jane seemed to know that it was time to bow out and leave me be. Like any wise teacher, she had done her job well and knew when it was time to bid me adieu. At that point, her voice blended seamlessly with my own thoughts.

Those types of thoughts are what we call self-talk, as were Jane's probing questions, compassionate comments, and whispered asides. I was fortunate to have her, because my belief in her was so strong that I never doubted what she said. I never could have had such faith in my own voice as a young child, or even as a teenager. I saw myself as too flawed (and I was), whereas, Jane was wisdom central, channel WISE on the dial, and I knew I could trust her completely.

Here are some of the things she'd say to me:

- "Aw, sweetie, I know it hurts, but you'll be alright."
- "I'm here with you. You're not alone and never will be."
- "You didn't deserve that."
- "I know that's what you think you want, but it's not good for you."
- "C'mon, let's get out of here."
- "Just cry and you'll feel better."
- "You'll see, I promise, it'll all turn out just fine."
- "You're okay, you're okay, you're okay."

Today I still marvel at her wisdom. Reading her words brings tears to my eyes. I didn't always listen to Jane's wisdom, but that wasn't her fault; she did her best to steer my life on a healthy course. During the first half of my life when I struggled with food—and life—I wish Ms. Jane Smarty-Pants could have pumped up the volume a bit more to save me from myself. I heard all her muffled suggestions, but they weren't always forceful enough to drown out my unhappiness and crazed obsession with food. Ice cream, even in an unopened container in the back of the freezer, can scream, "Eat me right now!" louder than anything else in the room. Even the thinnest crust of pizza left on your plate can cause such a ruckus that you can't hear the whimpers of distress from your bloated stomach. And the siren song coming from a garbage can overflowing with party food can suck common sense right out of your mind. I know you know what I mean.

My hope is that this book gives you the words to end your food and body struggles and that you'll hear them through a Jane (or John) of your own until they become your thoughts and self-talk. In previous books, I've discussed learning and following the rules for "normal" eating, resolving internal conflicts about eating and your body, learning effective life skills, managing emotions, and developing healthy personality traits. *Words to Eat By* complements them all by getting to the root of your food and self-caring problems: what you tell yourself day in and day out.

I know I'm making progress as a therapist or author when clients or readers say they hear my voice in their heads telling them that they're full and can stop eating, would be better off not stepping on the scale, will regret beginning another diet, don't need to dwell in the land of painful memories, or are fine being perfectly imperfect. Hearing my words in your head will be a great start to improving your self-talk. It will have to do until you hear your own voice, loud and clear, wise and unshakable.

Think of the words in this book as me leaning in close to you and whispering in your ear exactly what will be best for you in any given moment and in any situation that involves food, fitness, or body size. I have your interests at heart and know you deep down because I was once very much like you. I told myself what you tell yourself to cause your troubles with food. Then I learned what to say to myself to end my struggles and to have peace and sanity, whether I'm thinking about food or eating it.

Dysregulated eaters—those who have difficulty identifying enoughness around food—generally say the exact wrong things to themselves, which perpetuates their troubled relationship with food and their bodies. They need a new vocabulary, a new language of self-kindness and self-caring when the voice of their eating dis-order grabs the microphone and rants and whines from center stage, drowning out the voice of wisdom. My aim here is to be your Jane—to say exactly what needs to be said so that you will soon develop your own voice saying the words you need to hear to gently guide you toward a healthy mind and body.

When self-talk changes for the better, so does everything (and I mean *everything*) else—what you feel, what you think, and, most importantly, what you do. It's where transformation begins, syllable by syllable, word by word, phrase by phrase, forming a spoken path out of the depravity and despair of food obsession. As you create and follow this path, you'll have no desire to seek out other voices to better your relationship with food; your own voice will be enough and all you need to guide you.

When I was in the throes of dieting and bingeing back in the early 1980s, I carried around the book *Fat Is a Feminist Issue*, by British psychoanalyst Susie Orbach, everywhere I went. I needed it by my side in case I might be around food, which was pretty much any time. *Words to Eat By* is meant to be to you what that book was to me, my bible for how to respond to my food cravings and what to do instead of eating. This book provides the exact self-talk you need for eating well, keeping your body moving, and being compassionate to the image you see in the mirror. You might wish to modify some of my words and phrases, but if you don't want to bother revising your own versions, that's fine, too. The self-talk I've developed for you will do the trick.

Nothing could be easier. It's like having my eating-disorder therapist / "normal" eater brain inside your head because the book is at your fingertips. Just turn to the right chapter to deal with your problem situation—dining with diet-obsessed friends, battling an oncoming binge, responding to snarky weight comments, trying to sneak by holiday cookies in the break room without snatching one, or deciding if you're really hungry enough to eat a second helping of lasagna on a lonely Saturday night—and choose the self-talk that will guide you through the moment successfully. After a while, you won't even need to use this book because you'll remember words and phrases by heart. And that's when you'll know you're finally on the road to "normal" eating.

One caveat: You don't need to be perfect at self-talk. I'm not interested in having you parse sentences, getting hung up on how to phrase your thoughts. I'm interested in you developing and acting on healthier ones.

It helps to put your self-talk into the present tense and use the pronoun "I," although some studies advise that using "you" or your own name leads to greater success. It works better to state your ideas positively rather than negatively, because you never want to remind your brain of what not to do.

My aim is to help you search your heart and come up with the words and phrases that will make you passionate about taking better care of yourself. My hope is that you won't, like a good soldier, simply take my self-talk and make it yours unless you honestly have a heartfelt connection to what I'm saying. Part of the joy in developing self-talk is taking it on the road and discovering what works for you.

I've included "Thoughts to Munch On" questions and statements in each chapter to stimulate your appetite for delving more deeply into your self-talk and thoroughly digesting the material in this book. I also have included case studies to illustrate how complex this subject matter is and to help you recognize the necessity of cultivating healthy self-talk to promote healthy self-caring. My wish for you is that the ideas and words in this book stimulate your desire to speak wisely and lovingly to yourself and that they accompany you on the road to "normal" eating.

CHAPTER 1

The Power of Self-Talk for Better Eating, Health, and Self-Caring

(What You Say Is What You Get!)

There are a slew of books on self-talk—more than six thouszand on Amazon alone. And we all know that there are thousands of books published on how to eat healthfully, nourishingly, nutritiously, more sanely, and whatever else people call improving your relationship with food. There are even books on how to improve your self-talk to lose weight. However, this is the only book that provides readers who are striving to become "normal" eaters (definition forthcoming) with the *exact words to say in the moment when they are faced with immediate food, body image, and related challenges.* After all, in the moment is when we finalize our decisions around food and our bodies, no matter what thoughts and self-talk have come before. The best-laid plans aside, in the moment is when we make our choices that lead us either to reach and maintain our eating and self-caring goals or to go galloping off in the wrong direction.

This observation is supported by the work I've been doing for more than thirty years as a therapist specializing in eating psychology, which is the why and how of eating, not the what of it, aka nutrition. I've treated hundreds of clients who have dysregulated eating, and I continue to be amazed and saddened at how few know what to say to themselves to lead happy, successful lives, never mind make wise choices about the food they're eating or feel compassion for their bodies at any weight or size.

The importance of rational and compassionate self-talk is also supported by my own struggles with food half a lifetime ago. As a person who ping-ponged between being a highly disciplined chronic dieter and a world-class binge-eater, my old self-talk was exactly the opposite of what it needed to be for me to overcome the disaster that was my eating. It also was useless in stopping me from purging after overeating, until I went to a therapist who helped me sort out what was driving my urge to purge.

I learned from her that what I was saying to myself would almost guarantee that I'd continue my dysfunctional behaviors. Who knew? It's okay; I forgive myself because I didn't know any better. But when I began to learn what was useful versus useless in the way of self-talk, I immediately understood why I had been stuck for so many decades in unhealthy food-related patterns.

Consider this book a bridge to help you apply the principles of healthy self-talk to "normal" eating in particular and to self-caring in general. So what exactly is "normal" eating, and why do I put the word in quotes? It's an approach to feeding ourselves that has four simple principles, and all four must be used in tandem and in sequence (one then two then three then four) to produce a positive, comfortable, healthy relationship with food. Here are the principles, which you can learn more about in my book *The Rules of "Normal" Eating*:

1. Eat only when you are hungry.
2. Choose mainly foods that are satisfying and that you enjoy.
3. Eat with awareness of and response to appetite cues.
4. Stop eating when you are full or satisfied.

A word or two about "normal" eating. Many dysregulated eaters get confused about the difference between "normal" eating and nutritional/healthy eating. Make no mistake, there is a big difference. "Normal" eating is appetite-cued and focused on hunger, enjoyment, and satiation. Healthy eating is about food's nutritive value.

Between "normal" and healthy eating, there are four possibilities: (1) You could eat according to "normal" eating rules but choose mostly low-nutrition foods, which would make you an unhealthy eater. (2) You could choose mostly high-nutrition foods but over-eat or binge on them, which would make you a healthy but not "normal" eater. (3) You could eat neither according to appetite nor nutritional guidelines, in which case you'd not be a "normal" or healthy eater. (4) You could make mostly nutritious food choices and eat according to appetite cues and be a "normal" and healthy eater, which is the ideal.

What is self-talk other than, uh, talking to yourself?

That's about it. It's neither more complicated nor more sophisticated than saying to yourself silently or aloud what you're thinking. In fact, it's so subtle, that we often can't separate it from our thoughts. If you were to stop this moment and consider what you're thinking or feeling about reading this book, you might come up with, "This self-talk stuff sounds kind of interesting, but I wish she'd get on with telling me how to change my eating," or, "I just want to eat differently, not teach my brain a whole bunch of new tricks." Both would fall under the umbrella of self-talk.

Vironika Tugaleva, author of *The Art of Talking to Yourself: Self-Awareness Meets the Inner Conversation*, explains: "How you talk to yourself decides how you feel about yourself and others. It influences the choices you make about big and little things. It determines the actions you consider essential and the ones you consider dangerous, the desires you honour and the ones you repress, the plans you make for days to come and the lessons you learn from days gone. Your inner conversation decides the quality of each moment in your life; and beyond the quality of each moment, what else is there? What else matters?"[1]

From my experience, thoughts are general and nondirectional, and self-talk is aimed at getting ourselves to do or not do something or to think or feel a certain way. Self-talk is mostly unfiltered and often involves passing judgment on ourselves, such as when we say, "I'm so fat it's disgusting," or, "I'm so good that I passed up that fudge in the office today." In contrast, thoughts are often simply about a subject, such as thinking about and visualizing your body or that plate of fudge. We might even have musings about the fudge—how it looks and smells and will taste—but that isn't quite self-talk either.

I don't want to quibble about the theoretical difference between thoughts and self-talk. My intention isn't to give you a precise differentiation. A fine working definition of "self-talk" is *what we say to ourselves consciously or unconsciously that reflects our thoughts and feelings and moves us to engage in behaving or thinking a particular way.* For the purposes of this book, it might express body compassion or revulsion or nudges toward overeating or stopping when satisfied, weighing ourselves or sidestepping the scale, or heading off to the gym or staying on the couch.

I doubt it would be useful to parse the subject further, so perhaps we can agree that the purpose of self-talk is a way of calling attention to something or pointing our thoughts in a particular direction. Self-talk can be positive, negative, or neutral. For example, if you plan on baking an apple cake, you might cheer yourself on by saying, "This will be fun," bring yourself down by insisting, "My cakes never turn out the way they're supposed to," or take a neutral stance by musing, "I haven't baked one of these in a long time."

Do you have trash or treasure thoughts?

Self-talk may be conscious or unconscious, that is, we may intentionally say things to ourselves ("You can do it" or "I'm not hungry
right now, so I'll pass") or we may have no clue that we're thinking
a certain way and expressing self-judgment ("I can't control myself
around food" or "Who cares what I eat cause I'm fat already").
Self-talk motivates us to do or not do something, but we don't
always realize that's the case. Much of our self-talk is steeped in
fear, guilt, shame, and negativity, all of which may make us feel anxious. Self-talk is often a habitual expression of or reaction to life
("I shouldn't do this" or "I'm bad for doing that") that does nothing
to help us improve a situation. Improvement happens only when
self-talk is intentional and conscious.

For example, when grocery shopping, if you like apples, do you
mindlessly grab any old ones and toss them into your cart, or do you
take time to purposefully and carefully select ones that are fresh,
with no blemishes, and just the right ripeness for your taste? If a
thought came into your mind urging you to pick apples covered
with bruises and smelling of decay, would you buy them? Not likely.
Here's why: You'd recognize this mental prompt as destructive, not
constructive. Selecting unblemished, fresh apples would be to your
long-term benefit, while stinky, bruised ones would be nasty tasting
at best and harmful to your health at worst.

I call thoughts that are beneficial to you "treasures" and ones that
will harm you in the short or long run "trash." Treasures are keepers,
and trash can't be gotten rid of quickly enough. Whether you're buying a car, choosing a mate, or deciding on a career—or eating—you
want to think long and hard to distinguish between thoughts that are
trash or treasure. Trash thoughts are irrational, based on emotional
reactivity, and do not have your best interest at heart no matter that
they insist they do. They are rooted in early memories, trauma, and

dysfunction, hardwired into our brains as elementary, primitive survival skills, or they erupt from our ancient longings or habits. However, they have nothing to do with making smart decisions in the present. Treasure thoughts have lasting value and promote living your best life. They're rational and evidence-based, always consider consequences, and involve problem solving instead of emotional reactivity.

Not to harp, but it's crucial to understand that self-talk generally nudges us one way or the other. We might say, "I'd call Joanie, but she's probably too busy to talk to me" (discouraging calling), or, "I think I'll give Joanie a ring, and if she's busy, she can call me back" (encouraging calling). We might say, "I ate way too much, so the whole day's blown and I might as well eat whatever I want" (encouraging mindless eating), versus, "I overate a lot today, so I'll just wait to eat again until I'm hungry enough for a healthy snack or meal" (discouraging mindless eating). It's obvious which thoughts in each case are treasures or trash.

When I bring up the subject of self-talk, clients often look at me blankly and tell me they've never thought much about what goes on in their heads. This is evident to me, but a genuine shocker for them. That's the point: They've been driving the car while asleep at the wheel, and then they wonder why they get into so many accidents and never reach their intended destinations. Perhaps you, too, are asleep at the helm of your life and remain blissfully unaware of the voices in your head (your thoughts) guiding or pushing you this way or that.

Or more precisely, you listen to the voices and do what they say, but you don't listen to the fact that you're listening. Get it? Your self-talk is so automatic that you don't realize it's running the show in the background. Think of these voices as invisible hands that gently beckon you forward or pull you back, lead you out of the darkness or drive you further into it. Just because you don't hear your self-talk doesn't mean it's not blathering on.

The goal of this book is for you to make self-talk conscious and constructive and serve your higher purpose, which can happen only when you know it's going on and decide to make it work for you. Think of it as eavesdropping on yourself, purposely putting yourself in the position of hearing everything you're thinking as if your thoughts are on your mental speakerphone.

How do we learn self-talk, and why did I get stuck with such a crummy script?

The answer is that growing up you either didn't hear or didn't learn the kind of self-talk you'll be reading in this book. We develop the way we feel about and talk to ourselves from how we are spoken to and how our parents, family, and other adults communicated with each other and with themselves. To stretch the idea a bit, if your parents and everyone you knew spoke German, you wouldn't grow up speaking French. Monkey see, monkey do. Being the little mimics that we are, we take in and spit out what we're fed even when we're unaware that there's a learning process occurring.

Two dynamics are involved in learning self-talk: internalization and modeling.

In *internalization*, we use how others value us as a way to assess and decide how we should feel about ourselves. We take in their views of us, which is like hearing surround sound, and make them our own, unconsciously accepting that the way they treat us is the way we should be treated. If we are frequently criticized by parents or others for being higher weight or larger than they wish us to be, we begin to think that something is wrong with us. We absorb views from important others (including the media) and adopt their same valuation of us, as well as the way it is communicated to us, that is, often through criticism and shaming.

Consequently, this becomes how we talk to ourselves. If Mom called you lazy in an annoyed tone accompanied by an eye roll, you probably call yourself lazy in an annoyed tone and maybe even roll your eyes. If Dad insisted with a disappointed, grumpy sigh that you had no common sense, that's how you sigh and what you tell yourself when things go wrong.

In *modeling*, we unconsciously or consciously copy what our parents say and do. If Dad makes fun of anyone who's not firm and fit, we may absorb his judgmental attitude without thinking and make his judgments our own. If Mom drags herself over to the scale every morning, steps on it, and then cries and calls herself names for being fat, there's a good chance we'll soak up the negativity and shame she has toward her body and do the same. We may use others' exact words and tone, or we may alter it. Either way, we get the message loud and clear (often without even realizing that there's any communication going on!) that the way to feel about fat or high weight is bad, bad, bad and that the way to change it is to be critical and demeaning.

For example, due to sexist societal pressure, many of my clients' mothers were highly critical of their own bodies and didn't have a kind thing to say about anyone's body except when it—theirs or someone else's—was svelte. These mothers were hard on themselves in general and doubled down when it came to lacking a culturally acceptable body type. Whether they'd lost weight and fought to keep it off or struggled to no avail, they kept themselves motivated by disparaging fat.

If you grew up hearing this kind of criticism day in and day out, you likely came to absorb thinking thin equals good and fat equals bad as easily and automatically as you breathed in the air around you. Pressed to say what you were learning, it might be, "I get it: Thin is good and fat is bad, and therefore, my body had better be thin rather than fat so that it—and I—will be considered good not bad."

Or maybe weight or eating wasn't a big issue in your house, but you had to keep your room immaculate, get top grades, make the varsity team, play the flute first chair in the school orchestra, or maintain a neat or suave appearance. Your parents let you know that these tasks were crucial and that nothing less than perfection was acceptable by putting you down when you didn't meet their expectations or praising you only when you did. They shamed or humiliated you or yelled and punished you in various ways. Or maybe they told you or implied in nonverbal ways that you were just average, stupid, a loser, and bound to fail or that you wouldn't amount to anything, didn't deserve life's goodies, or didn't have what it took to be whatever they wanted you to be.

The more they applied those words to you, the more those words got tattooed on your brain. Or, to switch metaphors, they became a bell that you couldn't stop hearing clanging in your head. You naturally believed their words as truth and, over time, who could blame you for not being able to remember when you felt any other way about yourself other than negative? You didn't know that you were none of the things you were labeled—not a single one! You assumed, like we all do, that parents (and other relatives and teachers and adults in general) knew best and that you were wrong and foolish to disagree and that it was perhaps even not worth your while to do so.

So on top of using a strategy of negative self-talk to motivate yourself to improve, you actually came to believe that you were all the bad things that were said about and to you (and that you now say about and to yourself). And the more you said them to motivate yourself to not be something, the more you reinforced your lack of value and defectiveness. And round and round we go.

Now, years later, you're so used to hearing and telling yourself what's wrong with you that you've forgotten that anything was ever right and, moreover, you can't imagine ever truly seeing any aspect of yourself in even the weakest positive light. Your parents' (or grandparents' or siblings') negative words have snuck into your brain, burrowed in, and bolted the door behind them.

Honestly, negative, self-damning self-talk is not all learned from parents or relatives. Let's not forget our looks-obsessed culture, which talks a good game about compassion but takes a suck-it-up, no-pain-no-gain approach to success and failure. We lionize people who suffer to reach their goals and ridicule them for not trying hard enough when they fail. We worship winners and detest losers. Simplistically, we act as if everyone starts out on an equal playing field (which they absolutely do not in terms of finances, community, family, economics, and genetics, especially with the ethnic, racial, gender, and religious bias running rampant in our society), and then we laud the ones who succeed and shame the ones who fail.

No wonder people feel bad if they don't attain or maintain success and tell themselves that they're losers; might as well say it before someone else does. After all, it's not worth thinking well of yourself if someone's going to come along and slap you down. This is especially true of how our culture fat shames and harbors conscious and unconscious weight bias. So if you have negative things to say about being higher weight or larger than average, you may not have learned to feel contempt about your body from your parents as much as from this stigmatizing culture we live in. You may have picked up body hatred from living in our fat-phobic society—from the media, friends and neighbors, and sadly, from too many well-intended, weight-biased health care providers. You may have learned it early on in the neighborhood, schoolyard, or in the doctor's office.

One specific kind of cultural weight stigmatization comes from bullying. Here's how it happened to a client of mine we'll call Eric. Everyone in Eric's family was big-boned and tended to put on weight easily. His parents were respectful and loving to him, and he was active in school sports, especially tennis. Growing up, he knew he was larger than other kids in his grade, but he felt pretty okay about his body ... until the day he was walking home from school carrying his racquet and a group of older boys started to tease him about being too fat to run around on a tennis court.

Eric tried to explain that his weight didn't seem to matter because he'd won several tournaments, but they followed him all the way home yelling "liar, liar" at him. Every time he saw these boys in school, they'd sneak up behind him and snicker "fatty" or say "liar, liar." After a few weeks of being bullied, without telling his parents about the bullying, he asked them to put him on a diet, which started a lifelong pattern of weight cycling (losing and gaining weight) until he ended up in my office at nearly four hundred pounds.

These days bullying is common inside and outside of school and on the internet. Another client of mine was bullied for her chubbiness by her stepbrother. Her parents told her to ignore him or laugh off his comments, but she finally decided she would simply lose weight and swore she'd never be fat again. Eventually she stopped eating enough to support her body and was diagnosed with anorexia and bulimia nervosa. Thankfully, through years of therapy (with another therapist), she gave up her disordered eating. When I treated her, she was dealing with her teenage daughter's binge-eating disorder.

Thoughts to Munch On

- What family experiences formed your self-talk about your body, eating, and self-caring?

- What school, neighborhood, dance, sports, or cultural experiences contributed to your self-talk today?

- How is self-talk hurting you and your ability to take excellent care of your mind and body?

- What are three examples of destructive self-talk that you wish to give up?

Moreover, most of us have come to the point that even when we try to sort out what the best health advice is, it seems a nearly impossible feat. We feel as if we're at the mercy of "shoulds" and "shouldn'ts" playing bumper cars in our heads all day long, victims of an onslaught of messages from the media and medicine about what and what not to eat—and when to eat it, to boot. Every time we think about food, it feels like a burdensome chore, a make-or-break decision.

Everyone from the woman at the gym with the locker next to us to the assistant manager of our local health food store thinks they know what's best for us to eat or what exercise will burn fat the fastest. The latest diet book contradicts the ones before it, one scientific study undermines another, eggs are in then out then in again, as are fats and red meat. Even when we try to base our thinking and self-talk on solid facts and science, they dissolve or morph into something else. It's all too complicated and so we slip into default mode, believing that it doesn't matter what we eat, so what the heck.

How is what I say to myself important to my eating?

If what you think and say to yourself isn't the foundation for eating, then what is?

One minute you're at your home computer, on a tight deadline to finish next year's projected budget for your boss, and the next you're swallowing that last slice of key lime pie that was minding its own business sitting in your refrigerator. What happened? How did you ghost-walk to another room and do all that chewing and swallowing without realizing it? When exactly did you make up your mind to stop typing and start eating?

Although you might not have registered it, somewhere between calculating employee benefits and opening the fridge, you had a thought—or more likely a bunch of self-talk—that propelled you into action. Maybe it was "I have to eat that pie" or "I need a break" or "I'd better get that last piece of pie before someone else snarfs it down." Maybe you were bored doing the budget and itching for a break. Or maybe you were thirsty and went to the fridge for water but saw the cake and said to yourself, "I want it"—and so you ate it.

Remember that just because you didn't intentionally consider and formulate the thought and it didn't register, doesn't mean that you didn't have it. These split-second flashes that morph into decisions—a form of unconscious self-talk—move us to act as surely as when we deliberately and consciously mull over an idea and devise a plan.

Believe it or not, most of us have thoughts floating around our minds, if not a running dialogue, much of the time. A thought is an electrochemical reaction, and "experts estimate that the mind thinks between 60,000–80,000 thoughts a day. That's an average of 2,500–3,300 thoughts per hour. . . . Other experts estimate a smaller number of 50,000 thoughts per day, which means about 2,100 thoughts per hour."[2] Busy little brains we have.

If you're a food fanatic, many of these thoughts are about what to eat and not eat. You get a mental image of a cheeseburger and fries and fly out of the house to the nearest McDonald's, even though you'd meant to fix a healthy dinner for yourself. Or maybe you think of cake and dig through your cupboards to find a box of cake mix and decide to batter up, even though it's ten thirty and close to bedtime. You probably don't know why these thoughts popped into your mind, but they snuck in somehow and got you to do their bidding.

If we don't slow down and listen to ourselves because we're busy doing, we don't realize that we're talking to ourselves. Most of the time dysregulated eaters have lots to say about food, whether they're eating or not. They scroll through thoughts about what they ate and didn't eat, what groceries they should and shouldn't buy, what they weigh, and how they look. Some thoughts gather strength and elbow their way the front of the line, while others slip into the background and are never heard from again.

In general, what's wrong with my self-talk?

Stop and think about the things you say to yourself about food, eating, your body, and other people's eating and bodies. If you can't think of anything right off the bat, here are some ideas that will stir your memory:

- I look fat in this.
- This makes me look thinner. The color is awful, but I'll take it.
- I shouldn't eat this, but . . .
- I know the doctor said this is bad for me, but so what, I want it.
- I've been good all week, so I deserve to eat this.
- This tastes so good, I can't say no.
- I can't believe I haven't lost any weight.
- I can't believe I'm eating so little and have gained weight.
- What a blimp I look like. I'm embarrassed to go out looking like this.
- It's not fair that she can eat fattening foods and I can't.
- It would be a shame to waste this food, so I'll eat it.
- I'll start my diet tomorrow.
- I'd give anything to be as ripped as he is.
- I don't feel like making dinner, so I'll make do with a bag of chips.

Do you ever think any of the above statements or say them to yourself? If not, what *do* you think and say on these topics? Let's examine some of these comments and see how they may form the unhealthy foundation of your eating and attitudes about your body. Then you can decide what's wrong with your self-talk and understand how it irrefutably derails you from becoming a "normal" eater.

- If we tell ourselves that a food we ate is "bad" for us, we risk walking around thinking that we're bad people for eating it when we're actually the same good people we were before we ate it.
- By telling ourselves that we'd give anything to be skinny or ripped, we're focusing on one aspect of self—weight or appearance—and making that the measure of our value, ignoring *all* the things we are as well.
- If we eat a food based on feeling we've been "good" and deserve it, that says that sometimes we might not deserve it because we've been bad. But what does that mean? How do we or anyone become deserving or undeserving of food?
- Saying that we're ashamed of looking like a blimp and using it as the determinant of whether we can go out automatically and erroneously links high weight with shame and the necessity to socially isolate.
- When we think that being wasteful should override appetite, we're making an eating decision based on an irrational set of assumptions.

Thoughts to Munch On

- How aware are you of your self-talk about food and your body?
- Is your self-talk generally said to put yourself down or to lift yourself up?
- How much effort are you willing to put into transforming your self-talk?

If you've gotten the idea that your self-talk has not been constructive for a very long time but rather has been downright destructive, you are correct. Destructive self-talk has six elements that make it universally harmful and will practically ensure that you won't reach your eating, fitness, or self-caring goals:

1. *All or nothing.* Every time you start a sentence with "I'll never" or "I'm always," you're in the self-talk danger zone because you're caught up in either/or thinking. It's not so much the words that will sink you but the concepts behind them: success or failure, being all good or all bad, doing it right or wrong, perfection or worthlessness. All-or-nothing thinking is a setup to swing the pendulum of eating or fitness way too far in either direction and is based on childish, wishful, simplistic thinking, while adults are creatures who need to think critically about complex problems. Banish words like "never" and "always" from your vocabulary, eating and otherwise.

2. *Failure oriented.* Destructive self-talk focuses on what you don't want to do, but because of the way it's often phrased, it's unlikely to prevent you from doing that thing. For instance, you might say, "I will not eat that leftover lasagna in the refrigerator," lodging that image of the lasagna on the second shelf of the fridge in your head. Now practically all you can think of is getting your hands on the lasagna. You've given your brain the wrong information, so no wonder you go and eat it.

3. *Comparative and competitive.* In self-talk such as "I want to be thinner than she is" or "I wish I had his flat abs," you can hear a person drifting away from themselves, trying not to be who they are, and wishing to be a different self. This kind of focus is superficial and has undercurrents of envy, insecurity, and not being good enough. Wanting to be better than or more than others may indicate that you feel you're not okay or enough as is. There are more productive ways to express your desire to grow and succeed than comparing yourself to others, such as wanting to be a better, updated version of you.

4. *Moralistic.* Whenever you use the terms "good" and "bad"—especially related to eating, body size, or taking better care of yourself—you're not only succumbing to primitive all-or-nothing thinking, but you're also employing judgment where it isn't necessary or useful. You're hardly an angel because you forgo a Snickers bar, nor are you a devil because you eat one. What you weigh neither confers blessings nor predicts that you'll wind up in hell. Moreover, if you're like the dysregulated eaters I've treated (and the one I was for half a lifetime), the bossier you are with yourself, the more you want to rebel against your own demands and commands. The moral of this story is that ordering yourself to be good will often paradoxically make you end up acting exactly the opposite.

5. *Negative.* Self-talk that is negative, punishing, shaming, and cruel will only bring you down and depress you. If you want to ruin a perfectly decent day or mood, yell at yourself for everything you're doing or have done wrong. Dredge up major and minor things. Remind yourself that terrible things will happen to you if you overeat, don't go to the gym, and eat fast food all the time. The truth is that we don't know what will happen to *you* in particular. All we learn from scientific studies are aggregate conclusions. It's okay to be fearful about your behavior harming your health, but too much fear overwhelms us, fragile humans that we are, and paralyzes us into denial and inaction.

6. *Shortsighted.* Self-talk that is impulsive and gratification oriented is worse than useless; it's downright dangerous. Telling yourself, "I have to eat that cookie," "I can't stop bingeing," or, "I'm too tired to go to the gym," gives you no information except that you wrongly believe you lack free will and aren't thinking clearly—or maybe at all. Telling yourself that you

can't tolerate the discomfort of not having instant gratification will, more than likely, confirm your thinking. Self-talk that sides with impulsivity and compulsivity will never stop your eating problems; it's what's causing them.

In future chapters, I'll explain more about how deeply your words affect your eating and body image, and you'll see that changing what you say to yourself creates a healthier strategy for managing food and your body. What we say to ourselves overwhelmingly does, in large part, lead us to who we become. Since we can't shut off self-talk, aren't we better off choosing ideas and words that will build us a better future rather than ones that will keep us entrenched in thinking negatively about ourselves and promoting self-destructive behavior?

In chapter 2, you'll learn the basics of what makes for healthy and positive self-talk. You'll find lots of examples of constructive self-talk and can use them to write your own script for every and any situation. Once you get your thoughts and self-talk in order, you'll see how much better you'll feel about yourself.

●●●

Case Study: **Jillian**

Jillian is a twenty-eight-year-old, single, third-grade teacher. She was "chubby" as a child, dieted in her teens and twenties, and now is "miserable" about her weight. Her job is very stressful, and she and her colleagues often use food (in the break room or out at dinner) to relax and unwind. She's too tired at the end of the school day to think about food shopping or making dinner and usually stops for takeout, which she sometimes has polished off by the time she arrives at her condo door.

Both of Jillian's parents "battled" with food and weight, as does her brother. She's convinced that, no matter what she does, food will be the enemy and she'll never slim down. No matter how I try to help her shift her goal from weight loss to great health, she comes back to "hating my fat body." She attends therapy regularly but shrugs when I ask if it's helping her, saying, "Not really. The number on the scale hasn't changed."

In sessions, we often talk about her pessimistic worldview and self-talk, which is overwhelmingly negative and characteristic of depressive thinking: "Nothing's going to change or work, what's the point, why bother, and life is just one disappointment after another." Her feelings of defeat are based, in part, on her parents having died in an automobile accident when she was fourteen and she and her brother being sent to live with her mother's sister, who was depressed and lived paycheck to paycheck. Jillian missed out on a college scholarship, was disappointed at having to go to a state school, and expects the worst to happen every day. In her work at the school, she assumes that parents will be difficult and thinks that her principal will probably fire her because she says what's on her mind.

Each time I bring up the likelihood that she suffers from depression or, at the least, dysthymia and might benefit from talking about better ways to manage depression than food-seeking, she deftly changes the subject. She's afraid to hope and of encountering more disappointment, and she wants change to occur magically with little work on her part. Her typical script, in and out of my office, goes like this:

- I'll never lose the weight I want.
- I come from a fat family, so what chance do I have of being a normal weight?
- I have no energy to food shop. It's so much easier to sit in my car and eat dinner.

- You must have some clients who don't change. Well, I'm one of them.
- I don't have the patience to do all the things you say. I'll be dead before I learn to eat right.

Can you hear the downward tug in Jillian's words, the stuckness and despair? This is what she tells her brain each day. This is the food she feeds it, and then she wonders why she's full of misery and can't change. Here is some of Jillian's revamped self-talk that I've been encouraging her to use and that she's been practicing reluctantly in our sessions:

- I'll become healthier little by little.
- I'll take care of my body well and feel proud of my efforts and learn from my mistakes.
- I will practice food shopping and cooking and enjoy knowing that I have the power to change my mind and body.
- If other people can change their habits, I can, too.
- I have the patience to work toward developing frustration tolerance and any other skills I need to care well for my body.

Imagine Jillian's brain hearing this self-talk every day. Imagine your brain hearing it. It's can-do, change oriented, and about health, mind, spirit, and body—not weight. It shows insight into what's been holding her back and confidence that she can do whatever is necessary to reach her goals. Now that you're beginning to understand how your self-talk has held you back from taking care of yourself more effectively, you can keep an ear to what you tell yourself. Remember to just be curious and observe and to be kind to yourself, knowing you're at the beginning of a process that will change your life and your eating.

CHAPTER 2

How Self-Talk Triggers Trouble with Food, Fitness, and Self-Caring

(Hey, Quit Talking to Me like That!)

I'm going to ask you to be curious with me for a few moments—to put aside your assumptions about why, when, and how much you eat, and consider a new possibility. What if food isn't your major problem? What if there are other, less obvious issues in your life that make you turn to food as a solution? What if scouring the cupboards for and then eating anything remotely edible is only a symptom of other difficulties? I'm not making this suggestion to frighten you but rather to enlighten you—and to bring you the good news that you have tremendous, exclusive power to improve your relationship with food.

You can tweak your metabolism and up your activity level, but the truth is that the foods you eat mindlessly and binge on aren't going anywhere. They're not going to magically vanish from your office lunchroom or the section of the refrigerator where your housemate hoards her goodies. Supermarkets will not be whisking them off their shelves. Holiday parties, celebrations, and family gatherings won't suddenly stop being food feasts. And fast-food restaurants don't plan on ditching their menus to start serving only sprouts and protein shakes.

I understand that you feel powerless much of the time around food, which is ironic, considering that you have the ultimate weapon to manage your appetite and optimally nourish your body. That power, your self-talk, resides in you and you alone. There's no magic associated with it, it doesn't require high intelligence, and you need no one's permission to access it. There's no prescription for it and no postoperative recovery time involved. Although there are some things you can't say aloud (like yelling "Fire!" in a crowded—or uncrowded, for that matter—theater), you have 100 percent control over what you say to yourself. And that capacity alone gives you the power to heal your food and body problems and take better care of yourself.

I wrote this book because I fervently believe that *what we say to ourselves about food and our bodies is the major predictor of how we will eat and care for ourselves.* Our thought-words have the power to make things unimaginably better or unbearably worse. Words have the power to harm or heal us. They have the singular ability to decide our fate around food and every other facet of life.

Do I have self-talk about my self-talk?

Most of us do. Listen to what you say to yourself about what you're reading right now. I bet you've got some sort of monologue going on. Really listen and notice that your self-talk is on two levels. One is what you're saying to yourself: your words, your views, and your ideas. This is called primary self-talk. Your thought-words in response to it are called secondary self-talk, which is generally made up of judgments about your primary thoughts.

Here are two examples of primary and secondary self-talk that you might be experiencing right now:

- (primary) "How exciting that I have the power to change my eating based on what I say to myself." → (secondary) "Who

am I kidding? I always get excited about a new way to deal
with food, but nothing ever changes."
- (primary) "I'm nasty to myself, but I deserve it because I
  really eat badly." → (secondary) "See, I'm such a mess that I
  can't even be nice to myself."

In the first pairing, your hopeful self-talk gets torn down by
your judgment about not being able to change, which undoes the
original positive self-talk. In the second pairing, you've created a
double negative whammy: first, you say something unkind about
yourself, and then you follow it up with another remark den-
igrating yourself for being so unkind. I hope you can see how
this kind of verbiage can't possibly benefit you in any way, shape,
or form.

This dual process is similar to a related process called primary
and secondary emotions. It's important to understand them because
they, too, place a judgment on you, a memo to self from self. As
feelings often arise from self-talk, it's important that you be curious
rather than critical about what you say to and about yourself because
of the emotional judgments produced. Here are some examples of
how that works.

- You experience a surge of anger (primary emotion) at your mom
  for insisting that you come over right away for a visit when she
  knows you've made movie plans with friends. As soon as you
  get off the phone with her, you feel guilty (secondary emotion)
  that you refused her request and are taking time for yourself.
- You tell your new girlfriend that you love her and feel giddy
  (primary emotion) that you finally said the words. Then you
  experience a bolt of panic that she'll laugh at you for blurting
  it out, and you feel stupid (secondary emotion) for having
  made yourself so vulnerable.

Stop a minute and take note about what thoughts are swirling around your head right now about what you're reading. Do they indicate that you're staying curious and neutral? Are you denying that you speak negatively to yourself because, if you admit it, you'll feel ashamed? Are you angry that you've been so caught up in negative self-talk all these years that words have beaten you down to feeling despairing or depressed? Are you heaping on more negative self-loathing by telling yourself you're a bad person for speaking so unkindly to and about you, and that you can't change?

Before you continue reading, make a pledge that you won't use anything you read in this book to beat yourself up. Start practicing positive self-talk right now. If you read an example of self-talk that you often use and want to say nicer things instead, simply make a mental note of it and move on. Refuse to get down on yourself. Use your power to observe without reacting. Don't dwell on what you've done or are doing wrong. Dwelling is simply a lousy habit, and the purpose of this book is to create new habits of speaking only positively about and to yourself.

You don't need to wait until you're finished reading to get into this groove. Instead, begin again. What a great phrase! It means that each time you do something and then stop and resume, you're creating a fresh start, a new beginning. Don't focus on the word "again" but rather on the word "begin." The focus should not be on looking backward; it should be on moving forward. We have an infinite number of chances to do better.

Before exploring useful self-talk for becoming a "normal" eater, you'll want to examine your current approach to speaking to yourself about food, your body, and self-caring in general. It's important to understand why specific self-talk is destructive. It's not enough to simply stop saying it because I suggest it will hurt you. Make sure you accept that negative self-talk actually takes you further and further away from your goals.

Read each self-talk example below, then answer why it will not only prevent you from becoming a "normal" eater but also will propel you onto a path of mega-dysfunction around food and your body. Unless you recognize and appreciate its dangers, and unless it frightens and turns you off (which it should), you'll continue to slip back into speaking to yourself in unhealthy ways.

I've divided dysfunctional self-talk into six categories: (1) food and eating, (2) weight/size, (3) change, (4) feeling defective, (5) emotions, and (6) activity/exercise. Remember that self-talk is sometimes just a thought and other times it's something you actually say aloud or to someone about yourself. One form of expression is as detrimental as the other. For example, is it helpful to think or say, "Boy, she's thin. I wish I had her body and her life"? Whether you think or tell someone, the content is a criticism of yourself and implies that you're unacceptable as is. Put-downs keep you down, not lift you up.

Here are examples of negative self-talk used by troubled eaters. Remember not to judge what you're reading if you recognize some familiar thoughts or chastise yourself for thinking in unhealthy ways. Simply acknowledge that this is something you say without judging yourself and doing a number on yourself about it.

Food and Eating

1. Foods made with lots of fat and sugar are bad.
2. Only high-fiber, low-fat, and low-sugar foods are okay to eat.
3. I shouldn't eat foods high in fat or sugar.
4. I'm good if I eat only high-fiber, low-fat, and low-sugar foods.
5. I must finish all the food on my plate.
6. If I don't eat this food now, I'll feel deprived.
7. I'm entitled to eat this food because I had a hard/busy/stressful day.

8. I'm not hungry, but I'll eat this food anyway, because it may not be here later.
9. Food tastes good and eating more of it tastes better.
10. Throwing away food is wasteful and wrong.
11. I don't care if eating this food isn't good for me or if it makes me too full.
12. It doesn't matter if I eat this.
13. I'd better eat fast or I won't get enough of this.
14. I might as well clean my plate because I've already blown it by eating food that's bad for me.
15. If I don't eat all day, I'll be able to eat more tonight.
16. No one can tell me what to eat or not eat.
17. I want it, so I'll eat it.
18. I can't say no to food I love.
19. I can't say no to food someone gives me to eat.
20. It's not fair that I can't eat whatever I want.

Weight/Size

1. No one will want to date me at my size.
2. I can't be happy if I don't lose weight.
3. The only way I'll have the life I want is to lose weight.
4. I need to lose weight.
5. I have a really good life but being "overweight" ruins everything.
6. I'll never be healthy at this size.
7. My fat body is ugly.
8. My thighs are too flabby.
9. Why bother to buy nice clothes if I don't have a decent body to put them on?
10. No matter how much I succeed in life, no one will value me because I'm fat.
11. Fat people are gross.

12. I have no self-control or self-discipline.
13. I don't blame people for judging me by my weight.
14. When I'm thinner, I'll be happier.
15. I can't go to doctors because all they want to do is scold me about my weight.
16. I'll have gastric bypass surgery and won't need to worry about what I eat.
17. I hate my body.
18. Who would want to date someone who looks like me?
19. I'd rather stay home and be lonely than go out and have people judge my body.
20. I can't look at myself in the mirror because I'm so gross and it's too depressing.

Change

1. It's hard to change.
2. It's too hard to change.
3. I can't change.
4. I've tried and can't change.
5. I just don't have what it takes to change.
6. I guess I don't want to change enough to do it.
7. I wish change were easier.
8. I'd change if it were easier.
9. I'll try, but it probably won't work.
10. I tried, but it didn't work.
11. My eating is always going to be terrible, so why try to change it?
12. If I didn't love food so much, I could change.
13. I'm too old to change.
14. I'll never learn all I need to know about eating to do a better job with food.
15. It's too big a job to change.

16. I've changed but not enough, and I still have such a long way to go.
17. I give up trying to change because it doesn't matter what I do.
18. I've been here before and was eating okay then relapsed.
19. No matter what I do, nothing changes.
20. I eat well for a while, then I fall off the wagon.

Feeling Defective

1. I'm not lovable.
2. I think I'm lovable, but I'm not sure.
3. Nobody ever loves me back the way I love them.
4. There's something wrong with me deep inside, something defective.
5. I have so many problems, who'd want me?
6. I have so many problems, why bother getting healthy?
7. I can't bear getting rejected.
8. I can't stand feeling hurt.
9. It doesn't matter what I say or do, people don't care enough about me.
10. I wish I'd never been born.
11. No one would care if I died.
12. I don't care what happens to me.
13. I've tried to make friends, but I always get hurt.
14. I've tried to belong to groups, but I never fit in.
15. If I go to therapy, that means there must be a lot wrong with me.
16. I'm a loner and don't like or trust people.
17. When people get to know me, they don't like me.
18. If I were lovable, I'd have more friends.
19. Nothing ever turns out right for me.
20. I'm not good/smart/good-looking/talented enough and never will be.

Emotions

1. I hate feeling uncomfortable.
2. I'm overwhelmed.
3. I can't stand being confused or uncertain.
4. I'll never stop being depressed.
5. When I'm unhappy, only food makes me feel better.
6. If I'm anxious, I have to eat to relax.
7. Food is the only thing that helps when I need comfort.
8. When I eat, my bad feelings go away.
9. I don't want to ever feel bad.
10. I've hurt enough and don't want to hurt anymore.
11. Whenever I feel good, something bad happens or ruins my mood.
12. People always disappoint me.
13. I'm not good with feelings, and I don't like to think or talk about them.
14. Feelings hurt too much, so I'd rather numb out with food.
15. If I let people get close to me, I'm setting myself up for hurt.
16. If I don't use food to feel better, I'll fall completely apart.
17. I don't need antidepressants because I'm not crazy.
18. I don't need therapy and a stranger giving me advice because it doesn't work.
19. I'm a private person and keep my feelings to myself.
20. I need to be strong, not emotional and weak.

Activity/Exercise

1. I'm so out of shape, I'll never get fit.
2. I can't stand how I look in workout clothes.
3. People will laugh at me and at my size at the gym/pool/track/walking trails.

4. I hate to exercise, so I must be lazy.
5. When people stare at me, I know they're judging me for being fat.
6. People will wonder what such a fat, unfit person is doing working out.
7. People think it's dumb that I'm trying to get fit.
8. I'll look stupid pretending I know what I'm doing at the gym.
9. Exercise is too hard.
10. I don't have time for exercise.
11. I don't have money for any kind of exercise program.
12. I should exercise, but I don't like it, and I don't have the energy for it.
13. I used to exercise, but I still didn't lose weight.
14. If I didn't eat so much, I wouldn't need to exercise.
15. I get active for a while and then stop, and that's my lifelong pattern.
16. I'm always too tired or depressed to exercise.
17. The gym is too far away, and there's no place closer for me to work out.
18. I hate exercising alone, and no one will go with me.
19. Being physically active makes me hungry, so I don't do exercise.
20. I'll exercise tomorrow.

Can you see why each of these statements is destructive and toxic to motivation and success? If not, reread the statements with an eye toward recognizing their destructive power (then imagine the damage they cause by repetition). Remember, you're reading this book to change your self-talk to become a "normal" eater; recognizing why certain statements are unhealthy and unhelpful is equally as important as identifying ones that are healthy and beneficial.

So there you have it, a list of negative statements (not exhaustive, by any means) that dysregulated eaters eat and live by, which all but ensure they'll never get healthy or fit, take top-notch care of themselves, or have a comfortable relationship with food. Some statements may have a bit of truth in them. It's true that it *might* take courage to go to a gym when you're at a higher weight than many of the people there. It *does* take patience to hang on during recovery when you relapse. Being emotionally hurt certainly *can* be unpleasant. And making friends or joining groups *may* make us feel frighteningly vulnerable.

It's time to take a minute here to talk about pain in life. Emotional and physical pain are part of human existence. It happens, and there's no way to prevent it. We can try to dodge and reduce it, but there will always be more coming at us because such is life. Here is the only unhumorous quote I have in my office, from psychiatrist R. D. Laing, which beautifully sums up what I'm trying to say: "There is a great deal of pain in life, and perhaps the only pain that can be avoided is the pain of trying to avoid pain." He's telling us to choose our pain rather than try to avoid it. So for those of you who say you hate discomfort of the emotional variety, it's time to screw up your courage and allow yourself to be a bit uncomfortable in the service of avoiding other kinds of discomfort.

Alternately, there may be discomfort in change, but you don't want to be reminding yourself of that every minute of the day. That's not where you want your focus to be. Unpleasant things *can* happen, but pleasant things can happen, too, and that's the approach you want to take with self-talk. Honestly, when you buckle yourself into an airplane seat, do you want the pilots to be thinking, "Gee, ya know, this plane *could* crash today," or would you rather they think, "It's going to be a great, safe flight"? If you were trapped in a house that's on fire, would you want the firefighter to be dwelling on the fact that many people die in house fires or on being determined that you're going to be one of the lucky ones who get saved?

What is the "dasn't" mentality, and how did I learn it?

I remember my grandmother telling me what I "dasn't" do when I visited her. It's an antiquated word you never hear today, but she used it all the time. She was a sweet but highly judgmental upper-crust Manhattanite, and when I was around her, believe me, I minded my p's and q's. I was all too well aware of what to avoid doing, because she was always harping on what people "dasn't" do: dress in certain ways, do such and such in public, and, especially, be unladylike. Whenever I hear people bossing themselves around now and being judgmental, I think of them as having a "dasn't" mentality. Dysregulated eaters have it in spades. I did, and I bet you do.

As I described in chapter 1, we learn how speak to ourselves by absorbing the ways our parents and other relatives and adults talked to us, each other, and themselves. Remember, emotionally healthy people don't bully anyone, including themselves. If our parents or caretakers usually asked questions of us such as "Are you done with your homework?," or, "When are you planning on cleaning your room?" we might tend to do the same and give ourselves a gentle, neutral reminder. On the other hand, if they tended to issue drill-sergeant orders such as "Get your homework done now if you know what's good for you," or, "You'll sit and finish what's on your plate right now or no TV tonight," we unconsciously may have picked up their tone and the implication that we're bad if we don't do what they say. And now we likely speak to ourselves in similarly bullying ways.

If Mom missed an important work meeting because she over-slept then angrily called herself a "stupid woman," we might hurl epithets at ourselves when we make mistakes. If Dad frequently seemed disappointed in himself and said, "I should clean out my car, but I'm too lazy," we might also blame our lack of follow-through on sloth. The way our parents talked to each other also affected how we came to speak to ourselves as we do today. Maybe they called each other names or even cursed each other out. Maybe they bossed each other around using words like "should," "shouldn't," "need to," "have to," and "supposed to" and then got mad when their com-mands weren't followed. Maybe they screamed these words at you or at each other.

Much of the self-talk of dysregulated eaters is super bossy: "Do this, don't do that, you can't, you shouldn't, you're bad if, you're good if, be good." It sounds like you're talking to a child who has no idea how to take care of themselves and requires constant supervi-sion and instruction to do even the simplest tasks. But you're not a child; you're an adult who would benefit from cajoling, guidance, and enlightenment, who would do better considering what actions to take rather issuing self-commands to get things done.

Did you enjoy being bossed around as a kid? I've yet to meet anyone (including myself) who answered yes to that question. So why do you do it to yourself now?

I know why I grew up using bossy talk, because that's how I heard my parents and other adults motivate themselves and oth-ers to do better. Therefore, I naturally assumed and hoped it would motivate me. Although my parents were far from being bullies, they did have high expectations and were very critical of themselves and others. They were raised to do what they were told, and that's what

I was expected to do as well. And I did, which led to me growing into an adult with high expectations who proceeded to reach them by being hard on myself.

Are there specific words I shouldn't use in self-talk?

There are, and—guess what—one of them is "shouldn't." It's what's called an external motivator. You'll learn more about motivators in chapter 3. If you were in therapy with me, you would know that I harp a great deal on the language people use in sessions, especially on eliminating the word "should"—along with its bossy cousins "must," "ought to," "have to," "supposed to," "need to," and "shouldn't"—from their vocabulary.

Here's why. Regularly commanding yourself (as opposed to gently requesting or encouraging) to be different implies that you're defective and need to be fixed posthaste, reinforcing what you may already erroneously believe about yourself. Eventually you simply give up trying to better yourself, thinking, "Because I can't do what I should do, I'm no good." I cannot stress strongly enough how enormously damaging words like "should," "ought," "must," "have to," "supposed to," and "need to" are for your self-esteem and self-image.

Clients often say that they "need to change / lose weight / be more active," and I tell them that they're wrong and that there's only one thing they "need" to do in life—the same thing all of us must eventually do. Do you know what that one thing is? Some clients get the correct answer right away, and others are dumbfounded by the question. The only thing you or any of us need to do is die! You have no say in the matter, no choice. We'll all die whether we wish it to happen or not. It's compulsory. Everything else is optional with consequences. It is not compulsory that you lose weight, eat better, get top grades, or be a kinder parent. I know you feel pressure to take these actions but framing them as needs only ratchets up the pressure and raises your defenses; it does nothing to solve problems, get things done, or help you change.

So if there's only one need in life—to die—what do we call the other things we hope will happen? They are wishes, desires, wants, preferences, and whatever we would like to see occur. We prefer being healthy to being unhealthy, we want to take a walk because we feel better afterward, we wish we were kinder to our children because we can see on their little faces how badly our harsh words hurt them, and we desire to eat more nutritiously because our bodies feel better when we do and worse when we don't.

An excellent reason to eliminate "should," "need to," and their cousins is because we associate these words with childhood and with being good and bad. You're good if you do what adults tell you to do and bad if you don't. These highly charged words are considered shame-based because they're meant to induce shame in us as children to get us to do what adults want us to do. We're meant to feel that we're good or bad boys and girls in order to keep on the right side of our parents or elders. Using these words is the most common way of socializing children because it's quick and gets results (through shame and fear). However, it does little to help children figure out what they want to think, feel, or do and why they feel or behave as they do.

When we do things that we're told we should do "just because," we may be tickled pink with ourselves, especially when the behavior involves self-denial, self-sacrifice, or plain old discomfort. We may even feel morally superior to folks who don't do what they're supposed to do. On the other hand, when we do things others say we shouldn't do, we may get a kick out of being rebellious and going rogue, doing what we've been told not to do. Rebellion may feel great for a while, but then sometimes when we don't follow orders, we also feel ashamed. Moreover, we sometimes believe that we're gravely disappointing others when we fail to comply with their "shoulds" or "shouldn'ts," and then we feel guilty. This kind of good/ bad thinking can follow you around for life.

"Should" and "shouldn't" and their brethren are shame-based words that have no place in learning to eat "normally" or learning to take care of your body. They are not words that honor and respect you. They show no compassion or kindness or curiosity about why you're not doing something you say you want to do. In fact, using them is part of how you came to have self-caring problems to begin with.

One way to overthrow the dictator in you is to keep a log of how many times a day you say or think "should" or another command. Keep paper and a pen in your pocket, or use your phone. Or wear an elastic band around your wrist and snap it when you decree that you must or mustn't do this or that. Notice how you feel when you say the word "should"—generally like a bad boy or girl in need of being chastised so you'll behave better.

The very good news is that you're not bad and don't require a verbal spanking to be a better person. Albert Ellis, an American psychologist and father of rational emotive behavior therapy (REBT), has a famous line about "shoulds" that says you would do best to stop shoulding on yourself.[1] Excellent advice to follow.

Replace self-commands with saying "I want/wish/prefer/desire/ would like to." These words come from the heart and, as such, are internal motivators. As you say them, take time to connect deeply with why you want to do something. Put your hand over your heart and say your want aloud: I want to take a walk, I prefer an apple to a lemon square (or in some cases, a lemon square to an apple), I wish to be healthy, I would like to find clothes that fit me better, I desire to stop weighing myself. This heart-to-word-to-action connection is crucial because it starts the ball rolling inside of you.

Let's face it, humans basically do what we want. We only command ourselves in order to nudge us along when we don't want to do something. As I often joke with clients, "If you won two million dollars in the lottery, would you really be saying, 'I should go to the lottery office to pick up my winnings'?" Of course not. You'd be out the door in no time flat because you want that money. Replacing external motivators with internal ones is a game changer for self-talk and for becoming a "normal" eater.

We always have a choice about what to think and say, both to and about ourselves. It doesn't matter if our statements are true because we can't know the outcome of a situation until it's happening or over. Demeaning, critical, shaming self-talk implies that you don't have enough desire to do something, so the idea is to boost desire. There are reasons you want to eat ice cream and reasons you want to not eat it. Ditto with going to the gym versus staying home and staying calm around your kids or bossing them around.

In chapter 3, you'll learn the basics of positive, healthy, constructive self-talk. For now, listen to how you speak to and about yourself and notice how often you use external motivators. Then practice using internal motivators. You won't do a perfect job. Sometimes you won't realize that you're using unmotivating words. With vigilance and diligence, however, you will eventually feel a shift toward wants, wishes, preferences, and desires, which will help you keep moving forward toward your eating and self-caring goals.

●●●

Case Study: **Sue Beth**

At thirty-seven, Sue Beth is a stay-at-home mother of four girls. Her husband, Joe, is away more often than not on business trips, and she runs a tight ship. Her daughters have daily chore lists and strict curfews. She admits it's hard for her when Joe is home because he teases her about being scared to break any of her rules, and she gets angry that his easygoingness sets a poor example for their daughters.

If there were such a thing as a rule machine, that would be Sue Beth. Her mouth spews out what's right and wrong day in and day out, whether she knows something about a subject or not. She strives to be clear about what's good and bad and acknowledges that she acquired the habit from her mother, who had embroidered quotes all over the house about *the* way to think and live. Her parents were both very religious and would often quote scriptures to her when they wanted to make a point. Her goal has always been to live the right way and avoid the wrong way.

With a hint of a Southern drawl, she explains that she eats mindlessly and sneaks all the foods she *shouldn't* eat when Joe is away, then is good when he's at home. She insists, "I know what I *should* be doing, so I don't understand why I can't do it. I'm smart, and I've never wanted anything more in my life than to be a 'normal' eater. What do I *need* to do to be more in control around food? Tell me what I *should* do, and I'll do it." Get the picture?

Here's a sample of her daily diet of self-talk:

- I should eat a salad, but I'm so tired of them. I'll just whip up some pancakes.
- I need to stop sneaking junk food when Joe's gone, but it tastes so good.
- I shouldn't have dessert ever because it only makes me want to binge.
- I have to get a handle on my eating. I'm such a bad role model for my girls.
- I ought to throw out all of the junk food in my house, and then I'll be good.

She finger-wags about everything, especially when it relates to what is okay and not okay to eat. Her brain must be like one long to-do list, listening to her good-versus-evil sermons. To replace it,

Sue Beth and I came up with self-talk that will serve her better because it will teach her brain to think more healthfully about food by moving her away from rules and toward her innate appetite cues.

- I will eat what I want, whether it's salad or pancakes, and I will do it mindfully.
- I will eat whatever I want whenever I want, no matter who is around, without feeling ashamed or guilty.
- If I desire dessert, I'll eat it mindfully without guilt, rebellion, entitlement, or shame and stop when I'm full or satisfied.
- I'm enjoying learning about why I make the food choices I do and will teach my daughters everything I've learned to help them become "normal" eaters.
- Foods are neither good nor bad but are less and more nutritious, and I'm not good or bad based on what I eat.

It was quite an adjustment for Sue Beth to do a "should-ectomy" and replace the external motivators she was in the habit of using around food with internal motivators or neutral words, but she gradually learned to do so. She said she stopped using "shoulds" and "shouldn'ts" so much with her family as well, and she was surprised that they did what was "right" more often than not, mostly because that's what felt best to them.

CHAPTER 3

Principles of Smart Self-Talk

(They're Right Here on the Tip of My Tongue!)

All you've been trying to do all along through eating is enjoy some pleasure, find comfort or relaxation, feel less depressed or lonely, and get over life's rough spots. However, besides compromising your health, the mental downside of your dysregulated eating is that you've likely been treating yourself in a punitive, moralistic, and shortsighted manner that has made you feel worse. Hopefully, you now recognize some of the mistakes you've been making in your self-talk and are eager to learn how to correct them. This chapter will give you the words—and the spirit behind them—to turn your eating around.

With every mouthful, you've been looking for hope or help, reprieve or relief, a sanctuary or sunshine to brighten your day. You didn't set out to have an eating disorder and not take the best care of yourself. This truth is crucial for you to internalize all the way down, into the deepest core of your being: *You never meant to hurt yourself with food.* Repeat this sentence aloud slowly, with some deep breaths in between repetitions, and let it sink in: *I never meant to hurt myself with food.*

If acknowledging this moves you, it's okay to cry, as sometimes happens when we give ourselves compassion. If you're feeling disappointed in yourself, sad, or even hopeless, it will pass. Wisdom and smart self-talk grow out of fields that are seeded with painful emotions. As you imagine the door closing on dysregulated eating, visualize another one opening wide on the wisdom and words you can use for the rest of your life to manage whatever comes your way.

At first, self-talk that is compassionate, accepting, validating, and loving may not seem as if it will bring you what you need quickly enough. Or you may believe you'll never be able to feel these emotions toward yourself. You might think you can feel them toward others but surely not toward your undeserving self. You'll have to trust me on this. You can and you will make these feelings part of you by opening your heart to them and letting them do their work.

As you learned in chapter 1, dysregulated eaters are overwhelmingly hard on themselves. Goodness, I know I was when I made impossible demands on myself to eat less or more healthfully or did a number on myself after eating too much. Sound familiar? Then I'm sure it will come as no surprise that smart self-talk is pretty much the opposite of what you've been saying to yourself for years. We might assume that you've had a self-talk problem all along, maybe even more than an eating problem. Making poor choices with food (and fitness and general self-caring) didn't happen because you lacked drive and passion to reach your goals; it happened because you didn't know what to say to yourself to achieve those goals and, sadly, primed by family and culture, took a common but wrong route that got you to where you are today.

I hope it's obvious to you now that the negative self-talk you've been using not only isn't helping you reach your goals but is also working against you. The critical self-talk you use every day reflects unhealthy, irrational thinking, makes you feel worse about yourself (and more likely to seek solace in food), and generates self-destructive behavior—just what you don't want.

What makes for constructive, smart self-talk?

Self-talk can be any old words or phrases, but constructive self-talk has six specific elements. The smartest self-talk encompasses them all, but please don't get hung up on making your self-talk perfect. There's usually enough perfectionism driving dysregulated eaters that they don't need any kind of nudge in that direction. Perfection is the last thing you want to push yourself toward. Instead, aim for consistency.

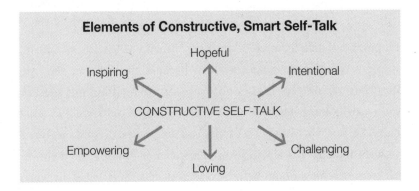

Elements of Constructive, Smart Self-Talk

Hopeful · Inspiring · Intentional · CONSTRUCTIVE SELF-TALK · Empowering · Loving · Challenging

Empowering

Empowering self-talk directs you toward doing the positive things you set out to do, such as getting exercise, filling your shopping cart with healthy foods you love, calling a friend when you're down, and stopping eating when you're full or satisfied. Correlating with and supportive of your goals, it has your long-term interest at heart. It's can-do, it cheers you on, and it makes you feel strong and proud (more on the must-have emotion of pride in chapter 8). It unsticks you from the past and transports you to a better future. It's the strong wind at your back as you sail courageously forward.

Examples of empowering self-talk regarding food, fitness, body image, and self-caring include:

- I have the power to nourish my body well.
- I am choosing to take a walk right now to get my body moving.
- I will show myself how strong I really am.
- I am passionate about reaching my goals because they're what I want.
- I will always choose to give my body love and compassion and to care for it well.

Hopeful

Hopeful self-talk ignores doubt and suffuses you with optimism. Its goal is not to predict certainty, because no one can see into the future; it simply chooses not to focus on anything but success. Forward-looking, it is based on tomorrow, not yesterday, about what could be, not what has been. It lifts you out of despair and brightens your outlook by introducing you to a world of options and a chorus of yeses, opening doors before your eyes. It fosters belief in yourself even when you have no proof that such belief is warranted— for example, by inspiring you to eat mindfully today, although you failed to do so yesterday and the day before. Self-talk infused with hope fills you with joy that things are bound to improve and are already changing for the better, because every moment holds new possibility.

Examples of hopeful self-talk regarding food, fitness, body image, and self-caring include the following:

- By practicing healthy attitudes and behaviors now, I'm creating a better future for myself.
- My thinking about my eating and fitness goals is rational and doable, and that makes them likely to happen.
- I get great pleasure and joy out of taking care of my body.

- This time next year I'll be proud of my progress with eating and healthy activity.
- I'll succeed in becoming a "normal" eater because I decided to take the smart road.

Loving

Loving self-talk uses ideas and words that underscore the message that you are lovable, precious, special, unique, and worth the effort to guide yourself in a positive direction. It comes from the heart and is directed to the heart. I can tell you that these are not the kind of thoughts that are usually floating around your mind. This kind of self-talk needs to be carefully crafted to embody unconditional love, compassion, kindness, and respect and to convey the message that no matter what you did or what happened to you in your life, you are imperfectly perfect just like the rest of us and deserve the best in life. We all deserve that best. Loving self-talk makes you feel that you've stepped out of darkness into shimmering light.

Examples of loving self-talk regarding food, fitness, body image, and self-caring include:

- I deserve to eat "normally" and have a healthy body.
- I do my best and embrace my imperfections.
- Loving my body means thinking about what works best for it in the long term.
- I choose loving myself over gratifying my urges and impulses.
- Loving me feels so wonderful, it gets me high.

Challenging

Challenging self-talk gently takes your hand and walks with you baby step by baby step toward your goals. It says it's just fine that you're going somewhere new and different. It takes you beyond where you've been and are right now into the future you've dreamed of. Its aim is to get you excited rather than anxious, which is what destructive self-talk does. Rather than let you stagnate, feel stuck, or drift back into old patterns, it gives you a gentle push to climb the next rung of the ladder or take another deep breath to help you cross the finish line. It doesn't overreach but knows just how much of a nudge forward you need. It poses exactly the right amount of difficulty for you: not so much that you might fail, and not so little that you won't succeed.

Examples of challenging self-talk regarding food, fitness, body image, and self-caring include the following:

- I can be brave and take small steps to grow, heal, and change.
- I will push myself a little each day to do what my body needs and not overdo.
- One day at a time, I'll take care of my body and my mind.
- Committing to exercise three times a week feels like just the right stretch for me.
- I'm excited to eat nutritiously and keep myself fit—really excited.

Inspiring

Inspiring self-talk makes you want to do what it is saying. Have you ever come across a character in a book who says something that makes you want to be like them or ever wished you could be like someone you admire? Inspiration comes from words said and actions taken by real people or fictitious characters. It makes us want to rise up and shout, "*I* can do that!" It makes our hearts beat faster, gives us energy, spurs us on to move out of our comfort zones, and raises the bar for us. It provides what therapists call a psychological shift, helping you see things in a different light so you can do things in a better way. It makes us want to become emotionally and physically healthier and lets us know we have a companion on our journey—best selves.

Examples of inspiring self-talk regarding food, fitness, body image, and self-caring include the following:

- If other people can get healthier, I can, too.
- Everything I do to take care of myself inspires me to do more.
- Doing workouts routinely is becoming easier and easier.
- I'm becoming a good cook—to my great surprise!
- Even the smallest gestures of loving on my body make me want to tell the world how great it feels and how much I deserve.

Intentional

Intentional self-talk has a specific purpose. It is consciously created with a goal in mind: to give you what you need emotionally in the moment and to move you forward in caring for yourself. You want it to be all of the above—challenging, loving, hopeful, inspiring, and empowering—but, most of all, you want it to make a beeline straight to your brain and heart pointing you in the direction of thinking and behaving positively. This means you will need to try out different kinds of self-talk to get just the right fit.

After a binge, you might wish to tell yourself, "That's okay. I ate too much. Tomorrow's another day." This self-talk is fine, but it's kind of ho-hum. If you need something more compassionate to take the sting out of your mindless eating, you might say, "I didn't mean to hurt myself. I'm doing better with food, little by little, and making real progress." Intentional self-talk comes from being conscious. It's not the drivel that seeps out of your brain when you're too tired to care. It's upbeat, to the point, and goal-oriented, and it assumes that great things are in store for you. And, most important, it won't take no for an answer!

Examples of intentional self-talk regarding food, fitness, body image, and self-caring include the following:

- While I'm watching TV tonight, I'll stay focused on the program and do nothing else.
- I'm leaving right now to go swim laps.
- I have enough energy to go grocery shopping and cook a great dinner.
- To relax, I'll experiment with three different ways to let go of tension.
- I'll have one slice of pizza and that's it.

Thoughts to Munch On

- Is your self-talk upbeat and hopeful?
- Does your self-talk include intention?
- Does your self-talk make you feel empowered to act?

Are there other components of smart self-talk?

We can learn the wisest ways of the world from books and other people. However, the most beneficial wisdom comes from seeing for ourselves what works and what doesn't. My clients with eating disorders are especially fixated on finding out how people in recovery got there. Yet, when those who've recovered share what they've learned, they (me included) are passing along knowledge from only their own experience.

Wisdom becomes real and useful only when it comes alive, which means taking ideas for a spin to see what they do (or fail to

do) for us. Mind you, you can't just drive up and down your drive-
way multiple times. You need to get out on the road with them
long enough to make serious decisions about whether or not they're
making a positive difference.

That said, there are qualities that we all need to be emotionally
healthy, and we can strive to incorporate as many of these qualities
into our self-talk as possible. They make us smarter, and acquiring
wisdom is what carries recovery along. A reminder: These are traits
for emotional health that everyone needs, not only people with eating disorders.

Self-Compassion

Most dysregulated eaters undergo a fierce internal battle when
someone tries to teach them to be more compassionate with themselves. If ever there were an emotion foreign to them, compassion
would be it. The majority are overly kind to others, cut them too
much slack, and will do practically anything to ensure that someone
doesn't suffer. Alternatively, they are wickedly hard on themselves
and are constantly saying things to put themselves down.

Here are some uncompassionate words that clients have called
themselves in my office: stupid, dumbass, hopeless, baby, big baby,
weak, and lazy. "Lazy" wins hands down as the word I hear most
often. A close second is hearing, "There's something very wrong
with me." I shudder to imagine what clients say about themselves
when they're alone. These denigrations roll off their tongues without their giving them a second thought. You'd think they might
be embarrassed hurling insults at themselves in front of another
person, but they're not because they (wrongly) believe they're true.

In reality, these clients are ashamed of who they are deep down,
and that shame manifests itself in the barrage of garbage they say to
themselves. They insist that it's the truth as they see it and feel a need

to say it about themselves before anyone else does. "Say something nice about myself," they snort. *"Why?"* They've so demonized their eating or weight or lack of fitness that they don't believe they deserve anything but twenty lashes—by their own tongues or someone else's.

According to Kristin Neff in her groundbreaking book *Self-Compassion: The Proven Power of Being Kind to Yourself,* compassion "involves the recognition and clear seeing of suffering. It also involves feelings of kindness for people who are suffering, so that the desire to help—*to ameliorate suffering*—emerges. Finally, compassion involves recognizing our shared human condition, flawed and fragile as it is."[1] To be self-compassionate, according to Neff, we need to first acknowledge that we're hurting, which means no more automatic "I'm fines" when we're in dire straits. Only then can we reach out a helping hand to ourselves to eliminate our suffering. It involves being moved by our own large and small sufferings and wanting to love—no, insisting on loving—ourselves anyway.

Now that doesn't sound so hard, does it? Then why isn't it a more natural stance with dysregulated eaters? If you can be kind to others, what's the big deal about turning the concept around and being kind to yourself? What indeed! Here are some possibilities:

You fear not being accountable.

One misunderstanding you might have is that compassion means letting yourself off the hook and being complacent about what ails you. *That is not what it means.* It doesn't mean you think you're perfect or are unwilling to face the music. It's not about condoning your mistakes. You can remain 100 percent responsible and accountable for what you do and still feel good about yourself rather than dislike yourself for your transgressions.

Here's how it goes: You recognize that you didn't intend to polish off a bag of Reese's Pieces but couldn't help yourself. If you could have stopped, you would have. You're not bad because of what you did. Instead, you recognize that you're unskilled at eating mindfully and at saying no to yourself around food and will aim to do better. You are kind to yourself because you're hurting, that is, feeling bad about the binge. Instead of beating yourself up, you develop a plan that includes de-stressing, learning to feel more comfortable around challenging foods, improving your self-talk, and eating mindfully.

You believe that if you do bad you are bad.

Another misunderstanding is that you *must* dislike yourself for your perceived "bad" behavior. Wrong. You can abhor a behavior but keep on loving yourself in spite of engaging in it. Ironically, when we make a boo-boo, we need more, not less, compassion. For example, you can be unhappy about hitting a fast-food restaurant on your way home from work but not feel disgusted with yourself. You can be disappointed at *what you did* but not be angry at *who you are* because you are far more than this one act of indulgence, even if you've engaged in it repeatedly. Though you stopped at the drive-through, you also graciously filled in last minute for a coworker, patiently helped your kids with their homework every night this week and found time to call your self-centered mother to check on her. The goal is to separate behavior from identity.

Fact: Without self-compassion, you won't become a "normal" eater. In truth, your eating disorder may stick around just to teach you this very crucial life skill. When you learn and practice it regularly, your eating will gradually become a good deal more manageable. I've experienced this happening repeatedly with clients: When they began being kinder to themselves, though their eating was as disappointing to them as it always had been, something changed within that made them want to take better care of themselves—and that was a turning point in their recovery.

You believe no pain, no gain.

Contrary to what you might think, research tells us that compassion-ate rather than critical self-talk improves and sustains motivation. This makes perfect sense. When we feel bad about ourselves, we want to retreat and give up on working toward a goal so as not to disappoint ourselves in the future. But when we feel good about ourselves, we want to keep going full steam ahead because we want to enjoy success.

You don't want to be a victim.

Self-compassion is not about feeling like a victim and walking around thinking or saying, "poor me." It's about sympathy, not pity. It's recognizing that everyone suffers in one form or another; that no one is perfect and was never meant to be and never will be; that we are not all born or raised on an equal playing field; and that comfort, not criticism or shaming, is the correct response to someone's pain—no matter what you learned in your family or from our culture. The whole idea behind compassionate self-talk is to remember that there are no good or bad people and that you can *feel* bad but not *be* bad.

To get your head on straight and view our human tribe as full of glorious imperfection, you might want to practice self-talk about this good/bad issue:

- Each act doesn't define me, and I'm more than my actions.
- There are no good or bad people, just frail and foible-prone human beings.
- No matter what I did that I think is wrong, I can make the right decision of being kind to myself about it.
- Life is messy, and I will feel okay about myself no matter what messes I make.

- I won't always make the choice that is best for me, but I can always be kind to myself regardless of the errors of my ways.

Specifically, around food, weight, and fitness you can offer yourself these self-compassionate words of comfort:

- No matter that I ate "x," I deserve to treat myself with kindness.
- Even if I didn't stick to my exercise schedule, I will speak to myself respectfully and with complete kindness.
- If I don't live up to my desire to be healthy, I will lift up my spirits by thinking about how I'm working toward that goal.
- I am allowed to make mistakes and not suffer shame and guilt for them.
- The worst thing I can do is not to overeat, but to mistreat myself for doing so.

Self-Acceptance

Similarly to how we've been taught that being kind to ourselves will dampen our ability and drive to reach our goals, we're also convinced that accepting ourselves means zapping all chance of changing. We've been told by culture and perhaps learned in our families to hate who we are and what we do—especially regarding our bodies—as a way to help us succeed. Wrong! Let's look at the word "accept," and you'll see why.

The word "accept" has so many conflicting definitions—from *receiving as is* to *approving of* to *assuming responsibility for*—that it's hard to know what's expected if you agree to accept your body. Does it mean that you approve of it or that you recognize it's yours but not as you wish it to be? No wonder self-acceptance is such a hard sell to dysregulated eaters. So let me be clear. When I encourage you to accept yourself, I'm not saying that you need to be pleased or content with who you are; I'm not asking you to view yourself "as is" as a finished product.

To "accept," in this case, means to acknowledge that right now this is your body and where you are—with eating, health, fitness, weight—without hating or bad-mouthing yourself. You want to be elsewhere but aren't there yet. This is how you look and how your body feels. This is how you're feeding and taking care of yourself during this particular snapshot in time. That's it. Are we good with that explanation?

You may dislike the message, but please don't shoot the messenger! Here's another way of looking at acceptance: imagine being lost in a forest without knowing it. You would likely wander around assuming you were on the correct trail back to civilization until you dropped from exhaustion. The turning point in finding your way out of the woods comes when you finally acknowledge that you are utterly and completely lost. Although you likely wouldn't jump for joy at this realization, by accepting the truth, you now have a shot at problem solving to find the correct path out of the forest. Accepting that you're lost is a precursor to finding your way out.

By accepting your eating habits, weight, or poor health, you're not surrendering to remaining as is; instead, you're paradoxically spinning off in a better direction to discover a more compassionate way to be with yourself when you're unhappy with your body or your eating, and so on. Here are some words of wisdom to help with self-acceptance:

- Being fine with what I'm doing now doesn't mean I won't or can't do better.
- I accept myself as is and will enjoy making progress as I change.
- I will accept however I am doing and always fight for improvement.

- Self-acceptance makes me feel like where I am is a starting, not an ending, point.
- I accept myself, flaws and all.
- I hold the paradox of accepting myself as I seek transformation.

Self-Validation

A common trait of dysregulated eaters is looking outward—for approval and reward, comparing themselves to or competing with others, yearning to be who they had been yesterday, and fantasizing about who they will be tomorrow. They're off gazing outward—Did I do okay? Am I okay? How do I look? Did I do enough? What do you think?—when they'd be better off looking inward. I know clients have validation issues when they start asking me questions about the progress they're making and get flustered when I turn queries back to them and ask how *they* think they're doing. I tell them that my job as a human being is to trust and validate myself and theirs is to trust and validate themselves. I let them know that, as their therapist, one of my primary tasks is to help them develop a strong inner capacity to self-validate.

I know from my work with clients that self-validation can be a tough nut to crack. In fact, I often share that it sometimes still requires considerable processing for me at the ripe old age of seventy-three to decide how I feel about something I've said or done. And I explain that sometimes I seek input from intimates to understand or make my peace with a person or situation. But I describe seeking feedback from others as far different than handing the assessment of yourself off to someone (or several someones) and accepting and living with their judgments. My approach is that I might get a bit of help from others, but ultimately, I get first and last dibs on what conclusions to draw.

This description of self-validation may come as a shock to folks whose parents were the overbearing arbiters of approval of their children's deeds. These folks, therefore, never learned how to validate themselves, are highly dependent, and lack life skills and self-trust. Additionally, people who grew up without sufficient parental guidance in childhood and were, therefore, left clueless and floundering on their own fear that asking for help means they're weak and dependent because being proud, for them, comes from independence. They do all their validating in their heads without getting reality checks from other people.

Moreover, our current other-oriented social media culture cruelly undermines self-validation. And it is not only kids, adolescents, and young adults being affected. Many dysregulated eaters in their thirties, forties, fifties, and beyond are still looking for approval from other people—teachers, parents, bosses, friends, lovers, spouses, and therapists—through grades, raises, promotions, compliments, praise, or social connections.

No wonder they have eating problems, because eating is all about trusting your appetite and ability to nourish your body. If you don't have the skills for effective self-validation, it shows up across the board. The good news is that when you develop these skills, they blossom in all areas of your life. With them *you* can decide when enough is enough, whether we're talking about food, work hours, relaxation, spending time with your children, or how much sleep to get. *You* decide what's best for you. How do you learn what's best? Like all of us, by trial and error. There is no shortcut or magical way.

Validation is about feeling that something rings true to you. Some things resonate, and some don't. Some are in sync with your beliefs and values and others aren't. Some speak to you in an unconscious way, and some leave you emotionally cold.

People might disagree mildly or vehemently with your thoughts or feelings. They may even denigrate you or shut you out of their lives. They may insist that their opinions are right or superior to yours or that they know you better than you know yourself. Hogwash!

You may want others to validate you so that you don't need to experience being wrong or failing by your own hand. You worry: Should I eat this or that? Are my thighs too fat? Should I get a hair transplant? What do I want to be when I grow up? Should I send the kids to private school? Must I let my sick, elderly mother move in with me? If we let others decide what's best for us, we can blame them when things go wrong. Self-validation can be scary, but it's also empowering and crucial for learning about yourself and for being a mentally healthy, autonomous person.

I vividly recall, though it was some forty years ago, reading the groundbreaking antidiet book *Fat Is a Feminist Issue*. I'd be sitting at a restaurant with diet-obsessed friends who'd be munching away on bowls of corn chips while chastising themselves for doing so. Whenever I could get a word in edgewise, I'd read parts of the book aloud to them about why diets don't work long term. I was the only one of my friends who took the antidiet path. *Fat Is a Feminist Issue* resonated loudly with something I knew as truth because I had been on many diets: They don't work. I hated them, and I never wanted to diet again. My friends thought I was crazy, but it turns out that following the principles of that book was one of the smartest steps I ever took in my life to become emotionally healthy.

Self-validation is predicated on trusting yourself, which is based on self-attunement or knowing what you feel and think. How can you say, "Yes, this is best for me," or, "That is what I want," unless you're connected to what's going on in your heart, body, and mind? The goal is to stay attuned to self twenty-four seven and be open to all thoughts and feelings. When you know what you're feeling and thinking, you make better decisions, have reason to trust yourself, and build confidence in your ability to self-validate. You can be open to other's ideas while still feeling secure that you know what you know.

To be attuned, the door must be open to a wide range of thoughts and feelings, comfortable or uncomfortable. All are welcome. None are turned away because they make you uneasy or uncertain. After all, self-doubt can be debilitating, but it can also, when channeled effectively, lead to insight and deeper self-knowledge. Self-talk questions that lead to attunement include the following:

- What specifically am I feeling—that is, what exact emotion?
- In what parts of my body do I feel it?
- Are my feelings strong, or are they vague and weak?
- Are my thoughts mixed, conflicted, or opposing?
- Are conflicted feelings making me uncomfortable, or do they feel tolerable?
- Are my beliefs, thoughts, values, and feelings in sync?
- What are my feelings and thoughts trying to tell me?

Self-Value, Worth, and Love

These traits are grouped together because they're so closely intertwined. (Can't you just see their arms encircling each other?) We love what we think is worthy. We value what we love. What we believe has worth gives it value in our eyes. There's no way to write about smart self-talk based on wisdom without understanding that the underpinnings of what we say to ourselves include how much we value ourselves, what we believe we deserve, and whether or not we love ourselves. But the truth is that we toss around concepts like love, worth, and deservedness in ways that distort the real meaning of these words.

Value

When we value something, we take care of it (e.g. our kids, our car, our favorite outfit, our childhood stuffed animal, the china set Mom

left us when she died, or our high school MVP basketball trophy).
We don't talk trash to or about it. We don't forget it has worth and
let bad things happen to it. We treasure it because it means the
world to us. We can articulate why we value it so much: There's
nothing like it, I've had it forever, I can't imagine life without it.
We're astounded or affronted when someone doesn't see value in
what's priceless to us. We don't care; what do they know?

People have rushed into burning buildings to save valued
objects, and they've spent lives obsessed about finding treasured
objects they've lost or that have been stolen from them. They've
written books and songs about what they hold near and dear and
how they'll never get over what they lost. They've given their lives
defending what they've held in highest esteem.

Do you value your mind and body with this same passion, sense
of urgency, and depth of attachment? Do you cherish them and
swear to protect them till death do you part?

Here's some smart self-talk to embolden you to value yourself
above all else. Is that really okay, you might wonder, to put myself
above others? It won't turn you into a narcissist, I promise. Being
willing to put yourself first is essential for "normal" eating.

- I have value no matter what I've done wrong.
- At any weight, I have as much value as anyone of any other
  weight.
- I will do everything in my power to show how much I value
  myself.
- I decide how valuable I am in this world, no one else.
- Valuing myself is getting more and more exciting.
- Valuing myself means taking care of my body and mind to
  the best of my ability.
- No matter what happens or what I do in life, my value
  remains the same.

- Because I value myself, I will speak only compassionately to myself.

Deservedness

Let's talk about what you think you deserve. Many dysregulated eaters have low self-esteem. Because they're not expecting to get much in life, their low expectations ensure that they won't—and they don't. Truth is, when you feel truly deserving of good things in life, you don't work to prove that you deserve them. You don't need to eat a cupcake to show you're entitled to pleasure. You go out and find pleasures and do enjoyable things that don't harm you. What you're actually proving when you eat mindlessly is that you *don't* believe you deserve to feel good, because feeling yucky is exactly what happens when you regularly eat for nonhunger reasons. Paradoxically, you end up driving home the point that you deserve pain and suffering, not pleasure. Crazy, huh?

Moreover, you show yourself and the world that you don't feel entitled to grab life with gusto, or you wouldn't settle for a measly cupcake. If you're like many of my clients, you put up with abuse and neglect—all sorts of chronic, high- or low-level mistreatment that you shy away from thinking of as inappropriate—because at heart you're not really certain you *are* deserving of love, kindness, respect, and happiness, and of being valued, nurtured, and taken care of. You turn away from authentic happiness and shortchange yourself while resenting doing so, and this anger drives you to eat as the only pleasure you believe you're entitled to. In short, by asserting that you *deserve* to eat when you're not hungry, you're saying that's *all* you deserve and nothing more.

Passing on that cupcake when you're not hungry, luscious as it looks and tastes, makes a bold statement of self-worth: I'm not settling for some crummy (pardon the pun) cupcake. I want more.

I insist on people treating me well, and I'm done making excuses for them treating me poorly. I'm putting myself first for a change. I intend to be as healthy and strong and fit as I can be, and I don't care what people want *from* me, because I know what I want *for* me.

To help remind yourself and tell the world that you deserve the best life has to offer, here are some statements that reinforce the message:

- I deserve love, a long life, nurturance, health, fun, success, intimacy, happiness, comfort, care, and loads of laughter.
- I will stand up for myself when I've been belittled, taken advantage of, undervalued, shamed, or picked on.
- I am entitled to eat healthy, delicious food that nourishes my body.
- I have the right to move my body no matter what others think about my doing so.
- I deserve close and supportive friends, a partner who respects and loves me, work that is meaningful and satisfying, and to be treated like the class act I am.
- I'm entitled to earn enough money to support myself comfortably.
- I have the right to feel safe and secure.
- I will validate my own feelings and insist that people respect me for being a unique individual.
- It is my human right to get my reasonable physical, mental, and emotional needs met.

Remember, when faced with food choices, what you really deserve is laid out above. The question to ask when you don't know whether or not to eat something is absolutely not, "Do I deserve this?," because the answer will always and forever be yes, yes, yes. The right question is, "Will eating this help or hamper me from getting all the other things I want and deserve in life?"

Self-Love

Self-love must be a constant, a given, so much a part of you that it's like breathing. When I ask dysregulated eaters perhaps the most important question in therapy—"Do you love yourself?"—many stare at me blankly, some start to fidget, and others hem and haw before mumbling something like, "Well, yeah, I guess I do." Their responses are always far less than the resounding "Well, duh, of course I do" I always hope for.

The truth is that anything less than a full-throated "Yes!" won't do to generate the kind of self-talk that gets you to the gym regularly, makes you stop eating delicious food when you're full, prevents you from scouring the kitchen for anything that's edible when you're avoiding filling out your tax forms, or prods you along to the doctors' office for your annual checkup where you're likely to hear the same old song about needing to lose weight.

Not only must self-love be unequivocal, but it must be unconditional. That means you must love yourself at your worst when you feel the most disgust and contempt for whatever you've done and have utterly and completely failed to live up to who you wish to be yet again. It requires you to say, "I love you still" after every binge, whenever you stay home rather than go for a walk, a run, or a swim, in spite of binge-watching TV half the night and nearly falling asleep at work the next day, no matter that you forgot your sister's birthday, notwithstanding missing your last dental cleaning, and never mind buying all that useless crap on eBay.

The truth is that loving yourself wholeheartedly won't permit you to have a destructive relationship with food, because self-love and self-trashing are mutually exclusive. If you grew up being abused or neglected, you very well may not feel lovable today, but you may be unaware that feeling unlovable is driving unhealthy eating and poor body self-caring. You may wrongly believe that if you're a better person you'll love yourself, but exactly the opposite is true. You need that deep, abiding valuing and acceptance first; *then* you'll do right by you.

If you're having difficulty grasping this concept, you're not alone. Clients tell me they're unworthy of self-love because they behave badly, hurt others, harm themselves, and are lazy and imperfect. Well, so what? Every other person on earth has done the same or far worse, and they manage to love themselves in spite of these flaws. Our frailties are part and parcel of being human and are no reason not to embrace self-love.

If you want to improve your relationship with food, you have to make a choice, because I believe self-love is just that. You decide either to love yourself no matter what you've done or to love yourself only when you're closer to perfect. Those are your only options.

Unconditional love—not putting restrictions and parameters on when and how you are permitted to love yourself—colors everything, including how you eat and care for your body, and it triggers a positive, forward-moving process. Starting from the premise of self-love, you do good by you and feel more lovable, which supports treating yourself better. This process starts with thoughts and moves into self-talk, then into feelings and behavior. Here's some self-talk that promotes unconditional self-love:

- I will love myself every moment of every day for the rest of my life.
- Nothing I do can change my unequivocal love for myself.
- I may feel disappointed about or regretful of my behavior, but self-love will remain.
- Though I would enjoy emotional intimacy with others, I'm the only one who has to love me for my inner world to feel alright.

- I am lovable just as I am with all my defects, mistakes, and failures.
- Even when I act against myself with food, spending, inactivity, and poor self-caring, I'll still love and believe in myself.

Remember, we fight for what we love. We don't turn away or simply shrug our shoulders as if we don't care. Fighting is one way of standing up for ourselves. Another is to keep providing love, as a safety net, as a springboard for change, as a petri dish for growth. With self-talk based on the principles you're learning in these chapters, you are already facing forward. Now you just need to keep going.

What if I don't believe what I'm saying to myself?

I hear this lament all too often. The truth is that we're all faking it until we make it at times or, said another way, practicing till we get it (whatever "it" is) right. Think about the first time you drove a car after you received your license. Did you feel as if you were ready for the Indy 500 after taking a handful of lessons and going to the registry of motor vehicles? I sure didn't. Did you feel compelled to tell everyone on the road that you really didn't feel totally competent and were terrified that you might mow someone down, or did you just do your best to maneuver your vehicle and follow the rules of the road? When you start a new job, do you announce to everyone that you're positive the boss has made a terrible mistake in hiring you because you're actually totally clueless about your alleged expertise, or do you come in every day and try to be worthy of having been hired?

I understand that you feel like a fraud and a hypocrite and fear that someone will discover that you're not who you've made yourself out to be or who others think you are, and that you're terrified you'll fail and look like a fool for believing something that was so patently false. But the only way you won't succeed is by repeatedly telling yourself (and others) that you can't fake it till you make it. We're not expected to be 100 percent sure of ourselves when we're learning new information or behaviors. That's not how acquiring skills or knowledge works, ever. Having doubt is okay because everyone else has it too at times, even if they act as if they don't.

You don't need to be convinced that you'll succeed. Stop thinking that your words need to live up to your behavior. You've got it backward. You need to continue practicing until your behavior lives up to your words.

Not faking it till you make it is nothing more than a colossal failure of imagination. If we can imagine being a certain way—brave, calm, powerful, engaging—we have a good shot at becoming this way. Dysregulated eaters are terrific at imagining how they're going to fail, so I know you all have a major talent for envisioning. That being the case, it's time to turn your imagination around and, voilà, see your success.

To help you take on a power aura, watch the 2012 TED Talk "Your Body Language May Shape Who You Are" by Amy Cuddy, professor and researcher at Harvard Business School and author of *Presence: Bringing Your Boldest Self to Your Biggest Challenges*. She shows how deliberately changing our body language can improve the way we feel about ourselves and can even alter how others view us.[2]

Cuddy is wild about the "fake it" concept, substituting "till you make it" with "till you become it," because the more you do a behavior, the more your brain automatically adapts to doing it that way, and soon you simply do it the new way without much or any thought. Her focus as a researcher has been on body language, and she proves through experiments that we can use it to our advantage or disadvantage. In her talk, she shows us high- and low-power poses and explains how each actually changes the neurochemistry in our bodies. High-power poses (big, strong, open) increase testosterone, making us feel more powerful; low-power poses (small, weak, closed) raise our cortisol, making us feel more anxious.

She found that by doing certain poses for two minutes, people felt more powerful and less anxious. Imagine coupling power poses and new body language with smart self-talk. If you're standing in front of the refrigerator ready to do some serious mindless eating and you're in a power pose (think Superman and Wonder Woman) and telling yourself, "Whatever I'm looking for right now isn't in here" (an old favorite line of mine), you might be able to leave the fridge door shut and go find something better to fill your time and meet your needs.

You've learned how to make your self-talk smarter, more constructive, and based on wisdom. Now it's time to experiment with the concepts you learned in this chapter and see what works for you and what doesn't. Don't be afraid to try different words. I know in general what ideas and words will be helpful to you, but you will know which specific ones resonate only through giving them a try to see what actually moves you to change your behavior. I understand that you have doubts but please put them aside. Your doubts aren't going to lead you to success; smart, constructive self-talk will.

In chapter 4, you'll learn what to ask yourself to connect with appetite cues that will tell you if and when you are ready to eat, what foods would satisfy you, and how to eat mindfully and stop eating when you're full or satisfied.

● ● ●

Case Study: **Art**

Art—a recently divorced fifty-five-year-old computer programmer, with a grown daughter, Julie—came to see me after having had a triple bypass following a heart attack. He was terrified of dying, having been up and down the scale more times than he cared to count, losing and regaining more than one hundred pounds twice. His daughter found me online and encouraged him to call me, which he did reluctantly. He told me that he wasn't into therapy, preferred to work things out on his own, and was meeting with me as a courtesy to his daughter.

As I got to know him, he confessed that not asking for help had been a problem in his marriage with his ex-wife, Sarah, and that he supposed he could work on that along with his eating habits, which he described as "God awful. I put just any old thing in my mouth, never think before I say yes to food, eat fast, and am a member of the clean plate club. I only dieted to please my ex. It's been a free-for-all with food since she left."

He was a middle child, with two siblings on either side of him. His parents worked hard at two jobs each and didn't have much time for him. If his older brother or sister couldn't help him, he fig-ured out how to do it—whatever "it" was—himself, or it didn't get done. When I asked if he felt neglected as a child, he nodded and acknowledged that none of his siblings except the oldest one did a very good job with self-caring.

His self-talk sounded like this when we started working together:

- Listen, jerk-head, no more french fries, pizza, and ice cream for dinner.
- I look disgusting. No wonder Sarah left me. I can't believe she stayed as long as she did.
- What's the point of having heart surgery if I can't stop eat-ing garbage?
- I don't blame Julie for thinking I'm a slob and emailing me healthy recipes I'll never use.
- Tomorrow I'm going on a strict diet. Tomorrow. That's it.

Like most of my clients, Art didn't realize that what he was saying to himself was orchestrating his thinking and directing his behavior or that there were better messages to get his point, which was to become healthier, across to himself. Over time, Art found my help useful and maybe even enjoyed feeling cared about. He told me something therapists often hear from clients: "It was weird, like your voice was in my head." My ultimate goal, of course, was to have my voice become his voice and instill a whole new way for him to speak to himself, not only about eating, but about everything.

Here is some of the self-talk about food and his body that Art came up with in a homework exercise (he still preferred to do things by himself):

- I choose to eat healthy foods for dinner because they feel good in me, and I like myself better when I eat better.
- I want to look and feel healthy and will take care of this body for myself.
- I can ask for help or not, as long as the job gets done.
- I feel lucky Julie cares so much about me, and I will try making one of her recipes to prove it.
- I'll become a "normal" eater and get some exercise.

As a computer programmer, Art enjoyed the idea of putting commands into his head to get his brain to do something and wished he'd cottoned to this idea earlier in his life. Over time, he took up racquetball and said it was the perfect antidote for "sitting on my butt all day." Gradually his eating improved, and he got a kick out of telling people that he learned to eat better not through dieting, but by going to therapy.

CHAPTER 4

Smart Self-Talk about When, What, Why, and How to Eat

(Sometimes I Want Food So Badly, I Could Eat My Words!)

Now it's time to learn exactly what to say to steer your eating and self-caring in a positive direction. This means getting constructive self-talk going the minute you think about food before you can slip into autopilot and make ultimately destructive decisions that you can't reverse. Remember, constructive self-talk is the fuel that drives your progress. It needs to be empowering, hopeful, loving, challenging, inspiring, and intentional.

You might feel like you are helpless around food. It looms large, and you've given it a great deal of power in your life. Fact is, food is simply sustenance that often tastes very, very good. True, its biochemical structure is such that it does affect your brain chemistry and hormones, but that is nothing compared to a brain that is smart, a heart that is self-caring, and a will that is determined to put food in its rightful, limited place.

The eating process, from first to last thought about food, involves five choices or intervention points: (1) food thought, (2) food craving/choice, (3) conscious eating, (4) ending eating, and (5) post-eating check-in. At each of these choice points, you can move in a healthy or unhealthy direction based on what you say to your-self. Constructive self-talk will take you one way, and destructive self-talk will take you another. Remember that each choice point is another fork in the road, and you're in the driver's seat.

Choice Point #1: Food Thoughts

You notice vague or specific thoughts about eating or what you interpret as a desire to eat, which may be due to physical hunger, stress, or emotions such as boredom, anxiety, sadness, confusion, frustration, or loneliness. These thoughts just pop into your head and may come and go. What you say to yourself when you think you're hungry or have a hunger pang makes all the difference between responding to an authentic need for physical nourishment or going along with your brain, which may be trying to fool or seduce you into eating for some other reason.

Here are statements to consider and questions to ask your-self when you have thoughts about food and are trying to decide whether or not to eat. They will give you the answer to whether you're authentically hungry and it's time for some chow or you're just in a noshy mood that is more about emotions than actual food.

- How hungry am I?
- If what I feel isn't hunger, what else might it be?
- Am I hungry enough to eat, which is about "moderately hungry"?
- I want to eat when I have stomach hunger and not eat when wanting food is about something else.
- What is my body doing that makes me think I'm hungry?
- Am I feeling an emotion that's making me want to eat?
- I will eat only if I am truly hungry enough.

- Food will still be available later when I'm hungrier, so I don't need to eat it now.
- I love feeling hungry and knowing I can feed myself effectively.
- If I'm not hungry, I won't eat.
- I'll wait until I'm hungry enough to eat and will enjoy food more.
- Feeding true hunger is a normal, healthy, loving, self-caring behavior.
- When I nourish my body with food, I feel proud of taking care of myself.
- Am I bored, lonely, angry, upset, or procrastinating and not truly hungry?
- I'm fine waiting to see if I get hungrier, and if so, I'll eat.
- I don't need to run to food at the first twinge of hunger but can wait until I'm moderately hungry.
- No one can pressure me to eat when I'm not hungry, because I'm the only one who knows what my appetite is signaling me.
- I can decide whether I'm hungry enough to eat or not, and either decision is okay.
- If I wait until I'm hungry enough to eat, I'll feel proud of myself.
- I'm learning the difference between true hunger and mindless, compulsive, or emotional eating.

Choice Point #2: Food Craving/Choice

You experience longings for a particular food (with or without hunger) and thoughts about the pleasure you'll derive from eating it. The thoughts come and go or start and won't go away. You either make a food selection mindfully (with rational intent) or semi- or unconsciously (as if you're in a trance).

Here are statements to consider and questions to ask yourself when you experience food cravings and are trying to decide what to do about them. Focusing on these will tell you whether you have (1) a physical food craving that you want to acknowledge or (2) disordered eating thoughts that are trying to take over your mind and body:

- If I pay attention, my body will tell me what I'm in the mood to eat.
- It's okay if I don't have strong cravings because my body doesn't always know what it wants to eat.
- Am I having a food craving, or do I want to eat for other reasons?
- All foods, except for those I'm allergic to, are okay to crave and eat.
- I can respond to food cravings or not, because there's no right or wrong in having them.
- I will balance out nutritional and health consequences with what I crave to eat.
- Just because someone does or doesn't have the same food craving as I have, it doesn't make mine wrong.
- Even if I have a specific food craving, I can seek more nutritious alternatives.
- Just because I have a food craving doesn't mean I need to act on my desire.
- I know I have a food craving because I've been wanting this food for days.
- I'll have a bite of what I want, eat it mindfully, then put it aside.
- Having food cravings is a normal, natural part of a healthy appetite.
- I love managing my food choices by listening to what my body craves.

- I will politely decline food that people choose for me if I don't want it.
- I can proudly say no to food cravings for health reasons.
- Who am I eating to please—myself or someone else?
- If I'm not sure about what I want to eat, I can take my time deciding without feeling pressured by anyone.
- My body, my choice—period, end of story.
- I don't know what I want to eat, and that's okay, because maybe I'm not hungry.
- Am I eating this out of habit or emotional need or because I really want it?

Choice Point #3: Conscious Eating

You either eat mindfully with full attention and connection to appetite signals or eat mindlessly, including too fast, in a frenzy, with guilt, shame, or a numbness to feelings. Think of these as two ends of a continuum with attention/connection at one end and lack of attention/connection on the other. Knowing exactly where you are on the continuum is crucial to conscious eating.

Here are statements to consider and questions to ask yourself when you are eating to help you remain aware and attend to appetite cues:

- Does this food seem like too much, too little, or the right amount to eat right now?
- Am I eating slowly and tasting my food?
- I'm enjoying focusing on the taste and texture of each bite by letting food sit on my tongue.
- I'm fine being the slowest eater at the table.
- I will chew and swallow and rest between small bites at a pace that works for me.

- I'll enjoy eating mindfully even if the people around me aren't.
- Chewing and letting food sit on my tongue increases the pleasure of eating.
- Am I getting distracted, or am I giving my full attention to eating?
- I'll listen to what others are saying while staying connected to my appetite.
- Am I relaxed both in mind and body?
- I want to eat mindfully because it's as important as anything else in my day.
- When I taste individual flavors, I know I'm eating mindfully.
- Am I eating too fast?
- Am I enjoying this food?
- No matter what's going on, I'll continue to stay connected to appetite to know if I'm still hungry or if I'm full or satisfied.
- If my mind drifts from my appetite, I'll gently pull my attention back to food.
- I have a tendency to eat quickly, so I'll slow down to a snail's pace.
- I will always check in with myself to see how I'm enjoying my food.
- Every bite of food brings new pleasure—until it doesn't, and then I know I'm done.
- I look forward to feeling satisfied when I've had enough food.
- I look forward to feeling full when I've had enough food.

Choice Point #4: Ending Eating

While you're eating, you may notice that hunger is diminishing and that food is tasting less appealing. These winding-down eating sensations happen only when you eat mindfully—slowly and with attention on the food. If you don't, you're likely to overeat.

Here are statements to consider and questions to ask yourself when you're eating to help you know when to stop because you are full (have had a sufficient quantity and are no longer hungry) or satisfied (have enjoyed your food and know that pleasure in eating it has peaked).

- Did I eat enough food for my body right now?
- The goal of eating is to feed myself enough food to take away my hunger.
- I'm fine with leaving food on my plate.
- I can throw or give away food and feel okay about it.
- I'll stop when I'm no longer hungry, and that way I'll feel comfortable.
- Eating more won't help prevent anyone from starving anywhere.
- Less is more when it comes to eating because every bite counts.
- I can politely refuse food or extra servings of food.
- Am I enjoying my food and still feeling hungry, or do I feel pleasantly satisfied?
- I can be full and not satisfied or vice versa, both satisfied and full, or neither.
- Only I know when I'm done eating.
- I'll say no to food even if it makes other people unhappy.
- I can stop eating even when food tastes delicious.
- If I think I'm done, I probably am.
- Am I proud of myself for how I'm eating?
- Food flavor has peaked, so it's time to stop eating.
- I'm going to enjoy my next activity or the one after that as much as eating.

- Is feeling guilty, ashamed, or deprived driving me to eat more or less?
- I'm tuned in 100 percent to appetite signals about fullness and satisfaction.
- Now that I'm done, eating is no longer interesting.

Choice Point #5: Post-Eating Check-In

After you've eaten, you either may think about how nourishing, satisfying, and tasty the food was and how proud you are for eating mindfully, or you may feel guilty, ashamed, disappointed, and remorseful about how you ate on top of having the discomfort of an extended belly.

Here are some statements to consider and questions to ask yourself after you've finished eating:

- I'll check in with myself with curiosity and without judgment.
- How does my body feel now that I've eaten?
- Although I'm disappointed that I didn't stop eating when I knew I was full, I feel compassion toward myself.
- I'm proud that I stopped eating when I felt satisfied and no longer hungry.
- The food I chose feels so good in my body.
- The food I chose makes me feel bloated, so I'll choose better next time.
- I ate too quickly but stayed connected to my appetite, so good for me.
- I did a better job staying connected to my appetite than I've ever done before.
- Could I have stopped eating a bit earlier and still felt satisfied?
- Could I have stopped eating a bit earlier and still felt full enough?

- I wasn't hungry enough to eat, and next time I'll wait until I'm hungrier.
- I didn't do a perfect job, but I ate slowly and tasted my food, so good for me.
- I will think about being more conscious of eating and will practice more.
- I'm proud of how I ate a bit of dessert, then saved the rest to take home.
- I'm glad I shared dessert because that was just the right amount of sweetness for me.
- My body feels well nourished and satisfied and not the least bit deprived.
- I want to eat more often without any distractions.
- It's exciting that I'm learning to pay attention to my appetite.
- It's taking a long time to learn to eat intuitively, but I'm getting there little by little.
- I've made such progress in becoming a "normal" eater. Hooray for me!

These choice points are where the rubber meets the road. You have distinct moments—from when you first think about eating to the post-eating period when you're thinking about how you ate—to intercede and make sure you're heading in the best direction. What you do and how you feel about what you're doing depends on what you tell yourself in those moments. By making choice or intervention points conscious, you can intentionally consider how to move yourself toward "normal" eating. If you've been making food decisions without purpose and consideration of consequences, no wonder you've been unhappy with your eating. "I-Crave-I-Eat" is a recipe for disaster. Using choice point questions and statements will insert "I think" so that the process is now "I crave → I think → I eat or do something else."

Here's a shortcut to discovering if you really want food, which will make it easier for you to decide whether it's time to eat or do something else:

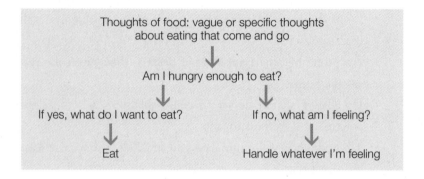

There are times in life when we need to be mindless, but around food is not one of them. Eating effectively for your mind and body takes attention and intention, which is knowing what you want to happen and then making sure it does. It's knowing your destination and then figuring out how to get there. It involves swapping out obsessing about food with observing how you're relating to it and problem solving to get the best results.

Thoughts to Munch On

- Which is your most difficult choice point with food?
- What is your easiest choice point with food?
- Where do you need more work—on attention or intention?

How do I get smart self-talk to stick in my brain?

Imagine if every time you thought about food, wondered if you were hungry, reached out mindlessly to grab something from the pantry, or started to feel full, you had nothing in your head but the constructive statements and questions above. What would happen if asking yourself these questions was as easy as breathing? What would your eating be like? What would your life be like? How would you feel about yourself? You'd be using rationality to make eating decisions.

One of the problems I see repeatedly is the opposite of this rational state of mind, which leads to mindless eating. Dysregulated eaters have (often unconscious) intense emotions *before* they eat and equally intense ones (regret, guilt, self-hate) *after* they eat, but they are unconscious in between. Emotions are high, and rational thinking is low or nonexistent.

Where's the adult who's supposed to be in charge? Often, nowhere to be found. Here's why. When you work hard and need to be conscious and focused most of the day, it's fabulous to rest your brain and decide to let it go off-line for a while to chill or recharge. However, you need to pick times when you expect that the higher-order-thinking part of your brain won't be needed, and then give it conscious permission to go off-line, knowing that it will be available if something comes up. The time for your brain to be snoozing is not when you're thinking about food or eating.

I can't stress strongly enough how important it is that we rest our minds adequately so that when we require their energy, focus, and rational brainpower, they're ready to roll. For example, consider how difficult it can be to pay attention to appetite and eating when you're wiped out due to stress or lack of sleep or nutrients. Even "normal" eaters have difficulty making eating (or any) decisions when their brains are begging to be put into sleep mode.

Another instance when it's hard to make food decisions is while we're preoccupied with a knotty problem, especially one that demands our immediate and total attention. In these moments, we're not thinking about why or how or what to eat, and without that brainpower, we often make poor food choices. When our brains are otherwise engaged, we can expect old habits to kick in—and if your eating habits are unhealthy, this is when you're most likely to float in a daze over to the refrigerator and consume most of the food in it.

The way to get smart self-talk to stick in your brain is to get enough rest, sleep, and downtime and practice, practice, practice.

Will practice really make progress?

You can guarantee yourself progress in engaging in constructive self-talk around food by repeating the statements and questions above, chunking them down into categories and knowing what you wish to say to yourself in each phase of eating. Practice is not reading this book and then letting it get buried under a dozen other books on improving your relationship with food and your body. You can't just read the self-talk in this book once and expect it to sink in. Practice isn't assuming you'll remember what to say at any eating choice point. How much you're determined to practice and how much you do shows how serious you are about becoming a "normal" eater.

Practice involves studying what makes for constructive self-talk, thinking about what you want to say in various situations, and then repeating the words to yourself or aloud. It includes jotting down ideas or memorizing a few statements and questions that will get your brain in gear. My advice is to repeatedly read over the self-talk you want to use for your eating daily or more often if you have the time. Memorize it if necessary.

You might wish to record what you want to think and say about food and play it back to yourself. Or make a list and tape it to the dashboard of your car to repeat at red lights, on the bathroom mirror to review while you brush your teeth, or on your refrigerator to deter you from making a mindless foray into it.

I'm not sure if practicing using constructive self-talk feels less than exciting or if dysregulated eaters believe it won't work, but in my clinical experience, they seem reluctant to stick with a practice schedule. They tell me they don't have the time or can't concentrate, or they start out gung ho and end up ho hum. Just like firefighters practice rescue operations on houses that aren't burning so they'll have muscle memory of the skills they need when they enter a house that's ablaze, dysregulated eaters must practice constructive self-talk when they don't need it so it will automatically spring to mind when they do.

Start a journal of constructive self-talk under different categories, beginning with eating. Put a list of compassionate statements and questions based in curiosity (not judgment) in your phone. Read them over when you're on hold, waiting at an appointment, or bored sitting in traffic. Read them rather than mindlessly texting friends about nothing in particular. Use these between times to better your capacity to eat "normally." Keep this book on your night table and read over what you want to say to yourself before you go to sleep. Pick it up when you awaken or have a power talk with yourself about eating as you're getting ready to start the day—and do it every day. The point is to keep constructive, smart self-talk and your intentions to improve your eating at the forefront of your mind.

Any more hints for improving self-talk?

Studying "the pronouns people use when they talk to themselves silently, inside their minds," University of Michigan psychologist Ethan Kross discovered that "a subtle linguistic shift—shifting from 'I' to your own name—can have really powerful self-regulatory effects." According to Kross, this shift can change how we feel and behave. His other idea is to replace the word "I" with "you" because it provides a sense of authority—of someone telling you what to do. These self-talk tweaks are certainly worth a try.[1]

Clients often use metaphors to tell me how awful their lives are. My job is to decode and reframe what they're saying so that they perceive whatever is happening as positive, not negative, or at least as neutral. Here are some reframings that you can use with your own self-talk:

- "I fell off the wagon" becomes "I was testing gravity."
- "I slipped" becomes "I temporarily lost my balance, but I got right back up."
- "I blew it" becomes "My eating experiment taught me what I don't want to do again."
- "I pigged out" becomes "I was exercising my intestinal muscle not my brain."
- "I went overboard" becomes "I took a little vacation and am back home now—to stay."
- "I lost it" becomes "I gained a lot of learning."
- "Everything is falling apart" becomes "I'm practicing putting things back together."

My personal favorite sayings or mantras that get me through the day (and night) include the following: *I'm doing the best I can, This is good enough,* and *This too shall pass.* These work to curb my occasional perfectionist tendencies and remind me that I have the power to manage my life. *I* get to determine what's good enough or my best, and I feel better assuring myself that most pain in life, emotional or physical, does eventually pass. No matter what you perceive is going wrong with your eating, these phrases will do the trick to calm you down and point you in a better direction. Repeat after me: *I'm fine, Everything's all right, I'm going to be okay.*

It's time to revolutionize your self-talk and start this minute to develop some kick-ass, can-do words and phrases that will bring you a sense of safety and security around food and a belief that you have the power to be the kind of eater and caretaker for yourself that you want to be. Remember, your relationship with food is only one aspect of how you care for your mind and body.

In chapter 5, you'll learn how to prevent a binge, stop eating when you're engaged in one, and how to speak to yourself with loving kindness and compassion, not recrimination, when the binge is over.

●●●

Case Study: **Luz**

Luz is a twenty-one-year-old pre-law student who was referred to me by her college guidance counselor. A straight-A student who also was captain of her soccer team and a champion debater, she exuded seriousness from the moment I met her. I could see right off the bat that Luz was used to being able to power through anything to get where she wanted to go. It was no surprise that she took this tack with "conquering" her eating problems and sought me out to teach her how to amp up her willpower so that she'd stop succumbing to food binges that left her exhausted, in physical pain, and hating herself.

She immigrated to the United States from Peru when she was six years old with her two physician parents when her mother got a prestigious job at a Boston hospital. She was a bright and curious only child, and her parents had high expectations for her. She doesn't remember a time when she wasn't trying to master some new task: English, the piano, or backgammon, which she played often with her father. Then came college, soccer, and debating. She was painfully hard on herself, self-critical bordering on abusive, and she had no clue what compassion meant for herself or for others. This was odd, as most dysregulated eaters overflow with compassion for other people but show little or no mercy toward themselves.

Luz's self-talk was brutal to listen to, and she clung to it for a long time because beating herself up had helped her achieve and excel in so many areas. She was frustrated and angry that her self-flagellation wasn't working around food and unhappy with me when I told her that willpower doesn't work well with biological imperatives (activities humans are hardwired to do to survive, such as eating and sex) so trying to enhance it was a waste of her time and mine.

Here's what she was used to saying to herself:

- If you weren't so undisciplined, you'd eat only what's good for you.
- If you weren't so lazy, you'd make decent meals for yourself.
- You're not trying hard enough to resist food that's bad for you, so try harder.
- What kind of person who cares about themselves eats like you do?
- You're weak, and that's why you don't say no to unhealthy foods.

Ouch! Most dysregulated eaters have a hard time with offering themselves compassion for their eating problems (or lack of fitness or high weight) because they fear that means they accept their behaviors as is. Luz was no different. We talked for months about how she could be kind to herself as is *and* still very much desire to change. Eventually, explaining the studies behind self-compassion as a motivator for transformation helped convince her that kindness toward her struggling, suffering self was exactly what she needed to learn and practice.

Here's a sample of the vastly improved self-talk, including some of my very own mantras, that Luz took with her when she moved out of state for law school:

- I am doing the best I can.
- I am patient and kind with myself as I move slowly toward "normal" eating.
- I deserve self-love and sweet words of encouragement to heal.
- I am imperfect and still love myself anyway.
- I know when to push harder to succeed and when to step back to understand why I'm not succeeding.

Luz's aha moment came when she realized that being self-critical was pushing herself further and further from her goal of "normal" eating and that she had to acquire a new skill to get there. She also learned that being a perfectionist, needing to win and succeed at whatever she attempted, and all work and no play were the perfect storm to generate an eating disorder. Additionally, we practiced stress-management strategies in session, which she recognized she'd need in graduate school and for the rest of her life, even "after I resolve my eating problems."

CHAPTER 5

Smart Self-Talk to Prevent, Manage, and Recover from a Binge

(I Get It—Word Power, Not Willpower!)

If you're reading this book, you probably know all too well what a food binge feels like: awful. If not, let me give you an idea. You feel as if suddenly everything has vanished from the world but food and there's a jumbo magnet drawing you relentlessly toward it. As if a piece of sourdough bread or a bag of Doritos is shouting or whispering your name over and over, and you've become laser focused on whatever food you're craving. As if you're being chased or hounded by some intense force pushing you forward and dead-ending you at the refrigerator.

Sometimes you don't even know what you want to eat except that the need to chew, taste, swallow, and fill up is overpowering. Nothing matters except your desire to put a particular or *any* food into your mouth—not your exhausted child begging to be tucked into bed, the overdue bills stacked neatly in front of you waiting to be paid, the party you're already fifteen minutes late for, or your favorite author's latest book that you couldn't really afford but just bought in hardcover to get you through another lonely Saturday night.

The urge to binge is like having an alien invade your body, succumbing to a waking trance, jumping off a cliff and not caring where you land, or diving into a raging river, never mind that you'll probably drown. You know from the get-go that this is dangerous territory you're dying to enter and that no good will come from acting on the impulse. But your yearning and craving ignore reasoning and off you gallop. The truth is that language utterly fails to describe the magnitude of desire to engage in a food binge.

The feeling is both frightening and seductive, comforting and exhilarating all at the same time. Frightening because you've lost all will and your executive mental processes have fled your brain and are not to be found. Seductive because you feel compelled to keep moving toward food with the promise of tasting something that makes you swoon. Comforting because food swears it will take away the pain and opening the refrigerator doors is like flinging wide the gates of heaven. Exhilarating because the mere thought of eating feels like loving someone so much you can barely stand it—and, even better, having them love you back just as much.

Are you saying that I talk myself into having a binge?

I am, and you do. Clients tell me that they *can't* help themselves, *have* to binge, and are *unable* to stop wanting to. They tell themselves the same lies. The truth is that we binge because our thoughts tell us to do so, which means we can use other thoughts that will tell us not to. Let's take a close look at the things we say to ourselves or others that push us toward food rather than away from it. These are the words on which I, a former world-class binge-eater, based my binges for decades. I'm proud to say that I don't even think about bingeing anymore and haven't for half a lifetime.

The good news is that you can prevent a binge, stop eating midway, and recover from one in such a way that will ensure that you will have fewer repeat performances in the future. For years you've been bulking up those neural pathways that cause you to binge and beat yourself up afterward. Starting now, by not taking these destructive thoughts seriously and by not acting on them, you'll allow these neural pathways to slowly die off. In their ashes, you'll rebuild a sound and wise internal dialoguing system that will make binge eating a thing of the past.

Whether you believe it or not, your fate is in your own hands—or, more accurately, in your own thoughts, because what you say (or don't say) to yourself from the instant the urge to binge pops into your head is the shaper of your destiny. The words you think and say, not food or your mood, are the determining factor of whether things go heads or tails up around food.

If you say what is rational and self-caring when you have the urge to binge, you'll talk yourself out of it. Oddly, if you're like most of my clients, your wayward eating has never been about food; it's always been about your spoken and unspoken thoughts unconsciously and consciously driving you toward or away from eating. They're at the very start of the process, while eating is at the end of it. If you don't believe me, go back and read chapter 3 about choice points. Without nudging yourself toward an eating binge, how would it happen? Food doesn't jump off your plate and into your mouth. It doesn't lie in wait for you in a vending machine and wrestle you to the ground when you happen to stroll by, shouting, "Ha, gotcha!"

By intentionally discouraging mindless or emotional eating, you ensure that it won't occur. Is it really that simple? Yes, it is. All-or-nothing thinking has conditioned you to believe that once you start eating, you can't stop. Not true. Let me prove it to you. If I put a gun to your head while you were lifting a slice of pizza or second helping of chicken nuggets to your mouth, would you not drop the food immediately? If someone said they'd give you $5,000 to not open the freezer and grab the Ben & Jerry's mocha fudge brownie ice cream that was your Saturday night date, would you not happily take the money and forget about screaming for ice cream? Of course you would.

So we know that you *can* stop if something is more important to you than whatever you're eating or planning to eat. Need proof? Haven't you restrained yourself from eating numerous times when you've stuck to a diet? That's because at the first thought of food, you've thought about something you wanted more: weight loss or good health. The point is that engaging in different behavior requires thought in the moment that blocks out food and pulls into full-frontal focus something that is more important to you—your health, pride, family, being comfortable in your body or clothes, or living your values. Repeating the specific rewards you'll get from not bingeing will remind you that there are many things you yearn for more than food; you just don't think about them as much as you think about wanting to eat.

One reward would be knowing how proud you'll feel when you don't get sucked into a binge or actually stop eating in the midst of one. I know pride may not mean that much to you right now. It doesn't seem like it could possibly have as much reward power as a croissant or a bag of chips. You'll learn more about how pride is the pot of gold at the end of the rainbow in chapter 8. For now, please understand that one of the reasons you haven't been able to stop bingeing is that you not only haven't rewarded yourself emotionally by saying nice things to yourself when you do manage to eat well but also you've come down hard, hard, hard on yourself for having binged in the first place. To stop a binge, you need to hoot and holler about the amazing thing you did—not eating or continuing to eat. Your focus must be 100 percent on having put down the food, never on having started the binge to begin with.

The only appropriate response to having binged—whether you stopped midway or continued until all of what you were eating was gone—is to shower yourself with compassion and praise:

- You binged because you were hurting, whether you knew it or not.
- You're trying to stop.
- You're far more successful than you used to be with overeating.
- Bingeing isn't a crime.
- You don't quite have the skills yet not to binge but you're getting closer.
- You're wonderful and lovable anyway.
- You're not perfect because no one is, but you're making progress with every bite of food you didn't eat!

Is that the kind of self-talk you've been using after a binge? That was a rhetorical question. I know how you think, I know how you speak to yourself. I was once one of you, controlled by food, led around by the nose, feeling hopeless to master my eating urges. I get that being hard on yourself comes naturally and that being self-compassionate is like speaking a foreign language. But unless you stop trying, you're bound to learn to do it in time. After all, you've gone the critical, self-abasing, hateful route, and that landed you in this book, so please, just try a little tenderness.

The thing about bingeing is that it's rooted in an obsessive-compulsive dynamic. An obsession is having intrusive thoughts about something or someone. The more you allow your mind to return to this thought, the higher your anxiety goes. Finally, you become so agitated that you convince yourself that the only way to get rid of your distress is to do something that will relieve it. And as soon as you do this thing—in your case, eat—your anxiety dissipates.

Consider your thoughts as feeding your anxiety or your anxiety as feeding upon your thoughts. The more you engage in compulsive behavior (food-seeking and eating) to reduce obsessive thinking (about wanting food), the stronger the link between them grows. Your actions keep your thoughts alive because they reinforce them.

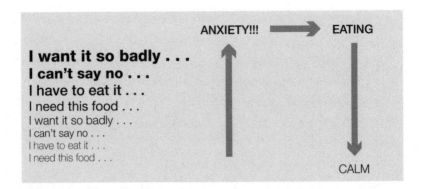

If you were simply willing to bear the anxiety that these thoughts bring (by self-soothing, or distraction), they would eventually disappear. Don't feed the animals!

Remember, neurons that fire together, wire together. Your goal with binge eating is to disentangle those eating disordered thoughts so that you can think that you want to binge but ignore the thought so thoroughly that it eventually slinks away because you're not paying any attention to it.

Here's self-talk that's made up of comments and questions that you require in order to stop bingeing behavior once and for all.

To Prevent a Binge

1. I'm not hungry, so food will not meet my needs.
2. What am I feeling that makes me want to bury the emotion in food?
3. I feel awful after a binge, and this time will be no different.
4. I have the power to take action to care for my feelings and emotional needs.
5. Rather than eat, I'll read / take a walk / sleep / play with the cat / clean out my car / text a friend / journal / have a good cry.
6. I will write about how I feel with the goal of managing my feelings.

7. If I binge, it's guaranteed I will feel miserable about myself: guilty, ashamed, helpless, bloated, sad, disappointed, and full of remorse, self-pity, and self-hatred.

8. By not bingeing, I will feel proud, wise, joyous, empowered, happy, and hopeful.

9. This behavior stops now, not tomorrow or the next day, but right now.

10. I will not eat, I will not eat, I will not eat.

11. I'm done with bingeing because it's something I used to do.

12. I can tolerate whatever I'm feeling because I'm an adult.

13. The desire to binge will pass because it has before and it will again.

14. I will not degrade my body by bingeing.

15. Nothing could make me binge right now.

16. I am in charge here, and my brain tells me that bingeing is a terrible idea.

17. I love myself too much to binge, and I'm tired of this struggle with food.

18. I'll feel so good when I awaken tomorrow and know that I didn't binge.

19. The idea of bingeing is a turnoff, and I can't believe it used to be a turn-on.

20. Bingeing hurts my stomach and my self-esteem and causes physical and emotional pain and harm.

To Stop a Binge

1. It's crazy to be shoveling food into my mouth like there's no tomorrow.

2. I'm perfectly capable of stopping eating now, so I will.

3. Put the food (fork, spoon) down now, right this minute.

4. I'm taking three long, deep breaths and giving myself a hug.

5. Enough. I don't want this food, and I don't want to be doing this—ever again.

6. What am I doing? I'm not even tasting the food. This is silly.

7. I'm walking away from the food now. Watch me keep walking.

8. Hey, everybody, I'm going to stop eating now.

9. Wake up—look at what you're doing to yourself.

10. What I'm doing hurts my stomach and my sense of pride.

11. Stuffing food into my body is a form of self-abuse, and I refuse to do it.

12. There is no magic way to stop bingeing. I will put this food away now.

13. It's only food, and my brain has tricked me into thinking it was something more.

14. I don't need to finish what I started.

15. I'm done with all-or-nothing thinking about food and resign from the clean plate club as of today.

16. I love myself too much to hurt my body and my spirit by bingeing.

17. I care about myself. I care that my eating is hurting me, I care so much about me.

18. I'm feeding myself pain, not comfort or happiness.

19. Bingeing is not an effective coping mechanism, so I'm stopping right now.

20. I can start eating and stop eating. Simple. I'm doing it.

To Feel Better after a Binge

1. What's done is done, and I will *not* beat myself up for it.

2. I wonder why I did that, what I was feeling, what purpose it served.

3. It feels so good to be kind to myself after a binge. Love ya.

4. I still love myself as much as I did before the binge.

5. Bingeing was the best I could do right now, and next time I'll do better.

6. I can choose how to react to my binge—be nice or be mean. I choose nice.

7. In this same circumstance, what would I do differently to prevent a binge?

8. I'll write down / record how awful my body feels so that I'll remember for the future.

9. I'm not where I want to be yet with food and feelings, but I'll be there some day.

10. I'll lavish affection on myself for the rest of the day and find something to do right now that shows how much I care about myself.

11. I won't eat again until I'm hungry, which will take a while and gives me time to do other things I enjoy.

12. I'll read more on binge eating and how to stop it.

13. By journaling, I'll feel better and maybe understand my bingeing.

14. There are many worse things I could do to hurt myself than bingeing, so I'm not going to think I'm bad for doing it.

15. Bingeing is just a coping mechanism I've used while I've been developing more effective skills.

16. I haven't binged in a long time, and I'm proud that it's become a rare behavior.

17. I'm disappointed in my eating and delighted that I'm not being self-critical.

18. Since I can't go back in time and undo the binge, I'll just move forward.

19. It's done, over, past, finito, bye-bye, so I'll put the binge out of my mind.

20. It's time to give myself the gift of meeting with an eating disorders therapist to help me stop doing bingeing.

Finally, during a binge, it's helpful to watch yourself eating in a mirror. Clients say that it awakens them to reality by seeing what they're doing. Plus, it provides a sense of what it would be like if someone was watching them. The secrecy of bingeing gives it a protective, seductive feeling, whereas being watched is a spell breaker. Try the mirror strategy. It can't hurt.

In chapter 6, you'll learn how eating well falls under the umbrella of giving yourself the best possible care you can. You'll be surprised that as your self-caring improves, so does your eating—and vice versa.

●●●

Case Study: **Gayle**

Gayle, a forty-one-year-old mother of two, was referred to me by her teenage son's therapist. Gayle's husband had died from lung cancer the previous year, and she was depressed over missing him. She was also tired most of the time from raising two children alone while working full-time as a case manager in children's services. The children's father, her first husband, was a no-goodnik and barely in their lives.

She told me right away that she had always been a bit chubby but had put on thirty pounds since her second husband, "the love of my life," died. Her daughter had just graduated from high school, lived at home, and had a retail job that she didn't love but took because she wanted to help her mother and brother out financially. Gayle's eighth-grade son had been skipping school for a few months and was in therapy, but she feared he was hanging with a "bad" crowd and getting into drugs and alcohol.

Although I viewed Gayle as a strong woman who was doing an excellent job with her children, she viewed herself as a complete failure. I saw a woman with two kids who'd divorced an abusive husband (who'd gambled away what money the family had) and then found and lost a gentle, kind man—and was still fighting the good fight. She saw only her mistakes: choosing her first "loser-of-a-man husband," believing she'd be happy for the rest of her life with her second one, feeling so exhausted after work that she wasn't spending enough time with her son to keep him on the straight and narrow, and not having enough money to put him in an after-school program. She even managed to see parental failure in her daughter not attending college right after high school graduation and instead settling for a mediocre, going-nowhere job to help pay the bills.

Her focus on the negative started in childhood. Her single-parent mother made her feel that she was never good enough: Why weren't her B's A's? Why wasn't she more popular? And how could she not know that she'd look better if she dropped ten pounds? Gayle focused on the negative because that's what she was taught to do. She wanted to lose weight, but now it was thirty, not just ten, pounds. She knew she could eat better but found food a too easily accessible comfort.

Her self-talk barely had a ray of light or sunshine in it and was clearly holding her back from changing her eating habits:

- I'll never look the way I want.
- Why bother looking good because who'd want an old widow with two kids.

- If I don't have food to look forward to every night, I don't have anything.
- If I lose weight, I'll probably gain it right back.
- What's the point of joining a gym when I don't have time or energy to go?

Gayle came into most sessions telling me what had gone wrong during the week: She'd overeaten several times, her daughter needed new tires for her car, her difficult mother wanted to come for a visit, and her son had been called to the principal's office again. I had to work hard to pull out of her the fact that she'd gotten a small raise, enjoyed four days of not overeating, that her son's grades were finally swinging back up, and that her mother was coming only for an overnight stay.

Here's what we came up with to put a positive spin on Gayle's life and possibilities:

- Life is manageable as it is, and will get even better.
- I have many things to be happy about and grateful for, especially my children.
- I have time and energy to eat well and nourish my body.
- I will take short walks every day and swim at the Y on weekends.
- I can do something about my eating, and I damned well will.

Fortunately, what is learned can be unlearned. Gayle understood that life can be hard but that she was making it harder and ensuring that she'd never succeed by focusing on her negative view of the past and not recognizing her successes in the present. She pooh-poohed the "fake it till you make it" concept but agreed to give it a try.

CHAPTER 6

Smart Self-Talk for Self-Caring

(Sweet Words Taste Better than a Hot Fudge Sundae!)

Poor self-caring and ineffective self-talk are at the root of most dysregulated eating. In fact, troubled eating is always primarily a self-caring problem. Very often, when that situation is reversed and you begin to value and appreciate yourself, eating becomes more manageable because your relationship with food and your body is part of the self-caring package.

Before I explain why that is and how easy it is to make your self-talk work for you, let me explain my choice of the word "self-caring." You may have wondered why I don't use the word "self-care," which is the noun folks commonly use when talking about taking positive actions toward themselves.

The word "self-care" seems too static and shopworn to me, too much like a one-off or a series of events without connection—dabbing on expensive cologne or treating yourself to a massage—whereas self-caring is an ongoing, active process. To me, treating ourselves well is not an action but a nonnegotiable mindset and continuous series of actions we choose because we can't bear the thought of living any other way. The goal is for these actions to become as automatic as breathing. This requires holding a self-view that says, "I will always try to do what's best for myself. So what if it takes time, bores me, scares me, puts others out, involves effort, means big changes, might be messy, or is new and challenging? Self-caring may at times feel selfish or defy the approval or pleasure of others. So what if it means saying no to others more often and yes more often to myself?"

Self-caring implies a flow of thoughts and behaviors, while self-care implies something you stop and start. Self-care can happen intermittently, while self-caring is the default of your operating system. You have one given job on Earth: to take the best care of yourself that you can. This does not make you selfish or self-centered; it makes you human, just like the rest of us. That's what all of us should be trying to do all the time. In self-caring, thinking about doing well for ourselves is the foundation of every decision and choice we make.

Why do we care about what we care about?

Let's return to the idea that began this chapter: Poor self-caring and ineffective self-talk are at the root of most dysregulated eating problems. When we love something dearly, deeply, and unequivocally, we throw 100 percent of our caring into it, whether it's a child, a car, a cat, or a career. We make sure to give the child everything we can to help them thrive, keep the car tuned and gassed up so that it's always in excellent working order, lavish almost as much love on the cat as we do on people, and always put our best foot forward at work.

When you care deeply about something, a normal reaction is to get upset when your cherished object is harmed or is hurting. For example, you might get distressed when your favorite jeans get stained beyond repair. It breaks your heart to see your dog limp around and suffer with arthritis. You'd give anything to make your child feel better when she's scratching away with chicken pox. You pick weeds in the hot sun and water your plants in the dead of winter because your garden has become a part of you and you feel responsible for keeping it alive.

The opposite is also true. When we don't love or care much about something, we generally don't put energy into fussing over it and don't give a hoot what happens to it. The ugly sweater that your aunt gave you that immediately went into the Goodwill box. The couch that's full of stains because you never liked it and bought it only because it was so cheap. The old clunker of a car you haven't put a dime into in years and hope will die soon so you can feel justified in buying a new one. Your grades in history because you want to become an artist and think studying what happened yesterday is a waste of time.

We don't intentionally hurt or harm what we care about. A case in point: I worked at a methadone clinic for six years and never met an addicted client who had a strong sense of self-worth. I'm not saying that clients' drug problems were only about low self-esteem, but I am saying that if they didn't doubt their basic lovability and valued themselves more, they wouldn't have begun and continued using drugs for as long as they did. It was truly amazing and gratifying to see how learning to value themselves made them so much more likely to take better care of their minds and bodies. Loving begets caring.

And so it goes with dysregulated eating. When you love yourself at full throttle in spite of your flaws and frailties (which we all have), you don't treat yourself like rubbish because it doesn't align with the way you feel about yourself. But, you may wonder, what about the chicken-and-egg theory? Do you not love yourself well enough and therefore don't take good enough care of yourself? Or do the results of your poor self-caring cause you to feel unlovable?

Fact is, some of us learn in conscious and unconscious ways early on, starting way back before we can remember, to neglect ourselves. As I said in chapter 1, how our parents took care of themselves, of each other, and of us forms the template for how we practice self-caring today. If you skipped this explanation in chapter 1, I encourage you to go back and read how modeling and internalization generate our core sense of self and how this core—for better or worse—is what dictates our thoughts, feelings, and emotions today.

Poor self-caring leads to ineffective self-talk, as if a line had been drawn directly from one to the other. You're not going to bother whipping up awesome self-talk if you don't take care of yourself in other ways. And ineffective self-talk promotes poor self-caring, which makes you feel worse about yourself and less likely to treat yourself well. Improving self-caring stops this vicious cycle—so does smart, powerful self-talk. By using it, you're far more likely to treat yourself as if you highly value yourself, which generates an upward spiral that keeps loving and caring escalating higher and higher.

As you learn to self-talk your way into managing your emotions, loving and honoring yourself for your uniqueness, becoming and staying physically active (to whatever extent you can), and being compassionate to your body while trying to improve it, you'll be amazed at how much better you feel about yourself and how your eating will reflect that newfound self-value. Self-caring is not the ribbon tied around the whole package; it's the gift inside. So as you become more effective in one aspect of self-caring, you'll become more successful in all aspects of it—including eating.

What can I say to manage uncomfortable emotions?

Emotional management and self-regulation are key components of self-caring. Too often people who've survived trauma, abuse, neglect, and other mistreatment were raised by parents who lacked effective skills for this aspect of self-caring and therefore never learned how to handle emotions, especially intense ones. Hence, today, these folks' eating disorders have become their pain-management system.

To reverse this process, you'll want to hold yourself in high regard. Does that mean being snooty and thinking you're superior to everyone else? No. Does it mean being selfish, not recognizing that other people have feelings and needs, and making sure that things always go your way? No again. It means valuing yourself as a unique—and, yes, imperfect—human being, nothing more and nothing less. Then, because you value yourself, you hold yourself in high regard and take care of what you cherish for all it's worth.

Here are effective sentiments you can reflect back to yourself regarding emotions in general:

1. I can handle any and all of my emotions.
2. Emotions are normal, healthy, and universal and are meant to help us navigate the world.
3. Feelings are bytes of information about what's going on in my inner world.
4. Uncomfortable emotions pass, coming and going just as enjoyable ones do.
5. Being emotionally strong means sometimes experiencing powerful emotions that make us feel vulnerable and bring us to our knees.
6. Emotions are neither good nor bad but value-neutral.
7. Emotional eating won't help me become a "normal" eater or a wiser person.
8. Emotions are neurobiochemical reactions that can be managed.
9. Experiencing an emotion isn't the same as dwelling or ruminating on it.
10. I'm okay and will be okay even when I'm disturbed deeply by emotions.
11. I am able to sit with an uncomfortable feeling and recognize it for being just that.

12. If other people can tolerate emotional pain or stress without eating, I can, too.
13. I feel proud when I experience emotions that used to be difficult to tolerate, and I no longer need to engage in comfort eating to handle.
14. I can tolerate any feeling alone or ask for comfort and support from others.
15. Food is not a comfort when I use it to feel better emotionally.
16. I'll experience this uncomfortable emotion rather than engage in mindless eating and feel disappointed in myself afterward.
17. I accept all my emotions without judging myself for having them.
18. The more I practice experiencing uncomfortable emotions, the less scared I am when they come to visit again.
19. I can't escape emotional pain because it's always there in life, but I can escape the pain of emotional eating and of running away from my emotions.
20. It's not weak to hurt or share my hurt due to emotions.

What do I say to love and honor myself?

Some people have difficulty with their *sense of self* or how they experience and perceive themselves. Basten and Touyz offer this definition of the term: "Sense of self can be defined as that subjective and continuous experience of being an individual, authentic person who is in control of their own mental and physical activities." They explain that "it is postulated in the developmental, psychodynamic and trauma literature that sense of self can be stunted by an environment of neglect, invalidation and trauma."[1]

If you don't feel authentic and whole, you may quash your true self in order to please others or fit in or may always wish to be in control and feel empowered. You might feel as if you have many selves and wonder which one you should honor—the one who gets straight A's in school or the one who sneaks food into his room at night? You might wonder which one you should love—the one who is president of a successful company or the one who finds more comfort in her refrigerator when she's lonely, as she often is, than in her husband and friends?

If you think your sense of self shifts and that you reshape your attitudes or behaviors when you're around others, you may speak to yourself in ways that reflect this perception. It may be hard for you to make mistakes and fail or to tolerate criticism, abandonment, or rejection. Self-talk that makes you feel whole through and through and have a solid, rather than a fluid, identity is crucial. Here are some examples of self-talk that reflect these qualities back to you and reinforce them:

1. I love myself, even though I make mistakes.
2. Everyone fails and makes errors, even people who are smart and successful.
3. My love of self stays the same whether I succeed or fail.
4. My love of self stays the same whether others think well or poorly of me.
5. I can't love and abuse my body with food at the same time, so I choose love.
6. Disconnecting appetite from emotions is part of loving myself.
7. I honor my appetite and my emotions equally, as they each serve a life-enhancing purpose.
8. No matter how badly people try to mistreat me, I will continue to love, honor, and take excellent care of myself.
9. Mindless eating was my best effort at self-caring before I knew better.
10. In learning to take care of myself, I don't need to do it perfectly.
11. I will surround myself only with people who I know love and honor me based on how well they treat me.

12. I decide what I'm worth, that I'm lovable, who I am, and what, when, and how much to eat.

13. As I take better care of myself, I respect myself more.

14. I don't need to be perfect (or eat perfectly) to love and honor myself.

15. I won't judge my worth by how well I do with eating, because that's just plain silly.

16. Other people have other problems, and mine happens to be eating.

17. Even if it sometimes feels weird and unfamiliar to love myself, I'll do it anyway.

18. I have the power to manage my eating.

19. When I feel low, I can trust carefully chosen people to comfort me.

20. If I need to pick self-love or mindless eating, I'll pick love every time.

What do I say to become and stay healthy and fit?

Eating in sync with body cues and mostly nutritiously is only part of self-caring. If you are physically able but not physically active, I would wonder why you're not taking better care of your body. Many clients tell me that they're tired or lazy, and my take is that this is the story they tell themselves that produces inertia. If they had a brain implant and awakened tomorrow with a different story floating around inside their heads, they'd produce different self-talk that would motivate them to become more physically active.

No matter what your size (granting that it can be more difficult to exercise when you are high weight), your body still needs care. Your skin benefits from sunscreen, and your teeth require cleaning. You need vaccinations, tests, and screenings to keep you healthy and prevent disease.

If you're not in the groove of body self-caring, here's some starter self-talk that gets to the root of the problem, which is you not valuing yourself sufficiently.

1. I accept my body as it is, and I still want to improve it.
2. I will focus on health not weight, in order to get physically and mentally healthier.
3. I can get healthier little by little, one small step at a time.
4. I want to become healthier and more fit.
5. I have realistic expectations about getting fit and healthy.
6. I feel so good when I take care of my body that it's a high in itself.
7. I'll find my own way to be engaged in activities that I enjoy.
8. I'll be active at whatever weight I am and won't care what people think of me.
9. I'll be angry, not anxious or ashamed, if anyone tries to make me feel bad about being physically active at my weight.
10. I can become fit without dieting or exercising like a maniac.
11. I'll go to the gym or out for a walk because I'll feel so good afterward.
12. The only way to succeed is through baby steps and more baby steps.
13. I want to be strong and flexible with reasonable endurance.
14. I'll go out and be active and be proud, not ashamed.
15. It doesn't matter what I wear to the gym as long as I'm comfortable in it.
16. I can make time to be active and find activities I enjoy.
17. A gym membership is not a waste of money, even if I go occasionally, if it's helping me become healthier.
18. Once I get into the habit of walking/biking/dancing/swimming/jumping rope, it'll be a lot easier to do it regularly.

19. I'll take that first step toward being more active and never look back.
20. I want to be healthy and fit more than anything in the world, and I have the power to do it.

What do I say to develop a self-loving body image?

Helping some clients with high weight to change their tune about their size and weight is one of my most difficult jobs. Aside from clients who are comfortable with their eating at a high weight, most seek therapy to lose weight or in fear of regaining it. Because our culture is obsessed with weight, many clients get upset when I encourage them to focus on health rather than weight. Some clients have difficulty getting around or being as active as they'd like, so they have a hard time shifting away from their most immediate concern, the heavy bodies they're carry around.

Nevertheless, over time and by recognizing the excessive importance placed on size in this culture and what it means in their lives, I can usually join forces with them to help develop self-talk that will support reaching their goals. We do this together by changing their negative thinking and stories about their bodies.

The following self-talk gives them an opportunity to decide how they want to feel about their bodies at their current size and what thoughts, phrases, and words will motivate them to be kind and caring to their physical selves.

1. This culture's obsession with thinness and weight loss is dangerous and destructive.
2. My goal is to take the best care of this body, whatever my size.
3. I have a choice about how to feel about my body no matter what anyone says.

4. No one can take away the self-compassion I feel for having tried to lose weight and having gained it back.

5. I'm done with looking at my reflection in mirrors and store windows.

6. I'll focus only on what's positive about my body.

7. It's time to think about enjoying life, not to dwell on the size of my body.

8. I'm very blessed with a body that does so much for me.

9. No more gazing at thinner people and wishing I were them because I'm okay being me.

10. I am so much more than my body, which is just my shell.

11. If people don't like my body, too bad.

12. If other large-sized people can enjoy life, I can, too.

13. I will focus on what my body can do, not what it can't do.

14. I will live as if I have the most precious body in the world, which is what I do have.

15. It's my business what I look like and how much I weigh.

16. If people tell me I need to go on a diet, I'll tell them they need to go on a retreat to learn to be a nicer person.

17. It's all about being proud of who you are, faults and all, period, end of story.

18. Sticks and stones can break my bones, but words can harm me only if I let them.

19. It's what's on the inside of a person that counts.

20. We all have an "as is" tag on us, so deal with it.

Thoughts to Munch On

- What do other people say that makes you feel cared about?
- What words or actions made you feel cared about as a child?
- Why would you not want to take excellent care of yourself?

Self-caring is putting self-love into action. Self-love is the engine that drives you, while self-caring is the wheels to keep the energy of that engine moving full steam ahead. If you're not sure that you love yourself, please don't wait around until you're more certain to take care of yourself. Instead, act "as if," which is a proven motivational tool for reaching your goals. As I argued in chapter 3, you don't need to believe what you're saying. Just say the darned words—over and over and over—and you'll start to believe them over time. This is exactly how you learned the destructive self-talk that's been leading you around by the nose until now. You kept saying things that were said to you, and eventually you came to believe them. They were wrong and, unfortunately, damaging and caused you mental and physical problems. Now you're learning new words that are more effective and will be the foundation for resolving these problems.

Act the way you want to be (and want to be seen), and you will become that person. After all, no one ever went wrong by thinking they were valuable and deserving and by taking excellent care of themselves, did they?

Are there images that will support my smart self-talk?

You can use smart self-talk by itself or, to enhance it, you can add word pictures. Some of you are more visual than others, meaning that you think in pictures and images. Even if you're not, consider using your imagination and adding a visual component to self-talk by employing similes and metaphors. In a simile, you compare two different things using the words "as" or "like" to connect them. A common example is "crazy like a fox" or "sweet as candy." In a metaphor, you make the comparison by saying something is something else, such as "she's a fox" or "he's candy to the eyes." Don't worry, you don't need to be an English major in order to use these elements of language.

Try this. Picture yourself as strong as a bull. When I say that to myself, I feel a tightening and centering in my core, and power coursing up from my legs. If I keep repeating it, I notice my shoulders rising and that I'm sitting up taller with my head held high and centered over my shoulders. Say "I am strong like a bull" to yourself several times and see what happens. Okay, now say to yourself "I am strong like a feather."

Do you notice the discord in your feelings, the confusion, and your body not knowing what to feel? "Strong like a feather" doesn't work. "Light as a feather does." If you want to feel stronger, you'd best not have thoughts of feathers floating through your head. If you want to feel lighter, however, leave the bull munching grass in his pasture, and look to the birds in the sky.

In hypnosis, you're sometimes asked to form an image in your mind to go with a new, positive thought. I use this technique (though I do not do hypnosis) with some clients who have difficulty expressing how they want to be in words. I ask them to think of an image that evokes whatever state they want to be in or feeling they wish to have. Many people choose an image from nature: an eagle soaring high above and looking down at the earth, a mountain towering above the plains, a tree tethered to the ground with strong roots, a river flowing over and around stones, a lion fierce and proud, a flower turning its face to the sun, or a serene cat content to be no one but themselves.

There are two ways to use images. Make a list of the traits you would like in yourself and match them with images. It doesn't matter if you think of the images as similes or metaphors. To fire up your imagination, here are traits to aspire to: being balanced, peaceful, calm, grounded, detached, powerful, untouchable, whole, or wise.

The other way to use images is to think about food and feeding and see what associations come to mind. Do you want to nourish yourself lovingly as a mother would feed her infant? Could you picture a buffet as an array of possibilities not necessities? What would be a hand-holder through a dark time, lift your heart, keep you company on a lonely night, help soothe uncomfortable feelings you're afraid of speaking, or distract you from mindless eating?

In my binge-eating days, I'd often picture a vaudevillian cane around my neck yanking me away from the refrigerator. Sometimes, I'd hook my finger into my shirt collar to drag me away from food. At dinner with a friend who ordered saganaki—fried cheese—in a Greek restaurant, I immediately had an image of boiling molecules of fat bubbling away on her plate (though I thoughtfully did not share this vision with her). A therapist I know tells his clients to think of unnecessary candy as chocolate-covered razor blades. You could picture fat balls clogging your arteries or sugar, like acid, eating away at your teeth. There are lots of creative ways to use images.

These are tools for taking care of yourself. *Remember to tell your brain what you want to feel, not what you currently feel if it's not positive and helpful.* Imagine taking care of yourself as if you're the most fabulous person in the world (which you are!). Brush away doubts and keep your eye on the prize: having the relationship with food and your body that you've always wanted, which is nothing more than what you deserve.

In chapter 7, you'll tackle how to eat in social situations—with friends, family, dates, or mates. You'll learn which self-talk makes "normal" eating harder and which makes it many times easier. All the situations you've gnawed your cuticles about will lose their formidability as you shift your self-talk from destructive to constructive.

● ● ●

Case Study: **Patrick**

Patrick is a thirty-two-year-old operating-room nurse who sought treatment with me to stop compulsive eating. He explained the following: If he ever took a rare moment to relax in the break room at the hospital and there was food around, he'd gobble it up in an instant. He said that he could go for hours at a time at work with a growling belly and ignore his hunger, but he added that when he isn't doing something, "I have to be eating."

Each night when he arrived home after his shift, he made a beeline for the refrigerator, even if the dog was barking her head off to be walked. He couldn't sit and watch TV with his partner, a "normal" eater, without bounding up every few minutes to get a bowl of popcorn or cereal from the kitchen or do some household chore. This behavior greatly annoyed his partner, who looked forward to the after-work time they spent together.

When I heard his backstory, his behavior started to make sense. He was the oldest of six children, with a father whom they barely saw because he worked three jobs and a mother who coped with motherhood by drinking. The family lived on a shoestring budget, and sometimes Patrick had to go begging to their neighbors for him and his siblings to eat. If and when his mother got a job for a month or two, he had to stay home from school to take care of his siblings. Often hungry, he gave food to "the little ones" rather than eat it himself.

It's not surprising that with severe emotional and food deprivation, Patrick became a compulsive eater, disconnected from appetite signals and his own physical and emotional needs. His self-talk spoke to these deficits:

- If I see food, I can't say no, no matter what the circumstances.

- If I don't eat when I'm not hungry, I may be sorry later when there's no food and I'm starving.
- There's always something to do, so it's not right that I sit and relax.
- Thinking about food and eating floods my brain so much that I can't think of anything else.
- I can't have all the pleasures I want in life, but I can always have food.

Patrick's brain has been reacting to food as it did when he was a love-starved and nutrient-deprived child. To update his reaction (and his self-talk), we discussed how his adult brain might fast-forward and respond differently to his adult life. Because he always had so much responsibility as a child, it's been hard for him to stop and focus on himself. Whenever he does, he feels guilty, anxious, and ashamed, and then he eats to squelch these feelings. For him to give up compulsive eating and become a "normal" eater, his self-talk needed to be about giving himself permission to relax, do nothing, and not take care of anyone but himself. It also needed to assure him that food would be easily available and accessible. With effort, he chose these words and thoughts:

- I enjoy time for myself.
- Food is plentiful and available whenever I want it.
- When food is around, I can choose to eat it or not.
- I honor my needs as I do those of others, because my needs are as important as theirs are.
- My appetite signals will let me know when I'm hungry and when I'm not.

As long as Patrick stays in the present and doesn't let his memories take over, he does better with food. When he puts his mind to self-soothing and tolerating the discomfort of changing his habitual thinking and behavior, his compulsivity and anxiety subside. With time and practice, his constructive self-talk will replace his destructive self-talk and become a default setting for healthier relationships with food, with himself, and with the people who matter in his life.

CHAPTER 7

Smart Self-Talk for Social Eating

*(It's Hard to Hear Myself Think with All
That Chewing Going on around Me!)*

Eating with others should be, at the very least, a pleasurable experience. After all, the ancient concept of breaking bread with people is about sharing and fellowship. Instead, for many dysregulated eaters, it's an exercise in self-consciousness, shame, envy, and off-the-wall anxiety. Rather than enjoying companionship and food, troubled eaters often are bracing themselves to be judged for their weight, food choices, and portion sizes. Sadly, a time for camaraderie may all too easily sour into a nightmare of distress and despair—and overeating from all the upset.

The fact that socializing these days happens so often around food exacerbates the problem many times over. For much of history, humans had tête-à-têtes over a cup of coffee or tea and took pleasure in making whatever they were drinking last or ordering a second cup or glass. Sometimes food was involved or even paramount, but even then, the major focus was on the social interaction, not the eating. When people did eat together, it was in their kitchens or dining rooms. Food choices were limited, and portion sizes circumscribed. Now we dine with a plethora of culinary possibilities and spend as much time thinking about what—and what not—to eat as we do actually chowing down.

In today's culture, it seems as if food is the focal point of every large and small gathering and conversation gets squeezed in between swallows. Plus, if you're dining at a restaurant, the food focus starts long before you get seated at your table. It begins with checking out the online menu or perusing the menus of several restaurants when trying to reach a group consensus on where to meet. Then, when you arrive, instead of sharing your latest exciting news right off the bat with friends or family (a marriage, divorce, move, baby, or promotion) you spend half your time roaming the menu, thinking long and hard about what is "okay" to eat and what is verboten, discussing your choice and theirs, having a lengthy conversation with the waitstaff about what's good or fresh, and obtaining a list of ingredients for each dish you're considering ordering. Doesn't *that* sound like fun?

You're not crazy if you feel as if you can't partake in social occasions these days without food being an integral part of the affair, if not its centerpiece. There's a breakfast or lunch spread at professional workshops, brought and bought snacks at sporting events, and now the cine-bistro concept of eating while film-watching. I've been on walks and short hikes with people who don't feel they can pack a snack for themselves without bringing *something* to share with the group. Not to mention attending two-hour board meetings (post-dinner hour) in which fruit, sandwiches, or pastries are delivered, as if our brain cells won't function without feeding them while we're learning or talking shop.

Why are social situations with food so difficult for dysregulated eaters?

Social gatherings with food can be a good deal tougher than solo dining for several reasons. One is because we're more concerned with having our say or listening to others than to attuning to appetite cues. Feeling full while seeing others continue to eat might make us think,

"Oh, what the heck" and polish off what's left on our plates just to be like everyone else. Or eating "forbidden" foods might cause dysregulated eaters to feel out of control about what they "should" and "shouldn't" eat and deny themselves pleasure. And it isn't just restaurants. It doesn't matter at whose home you're eating, the problem is that you can't control what will be put in front of you and fear that, whatever it is, you'll eat the "wrong" thing or too much of everything.

Alternately, some dysregulated eaters say they do better eating with others than by themselves. These are usually approval seekers and people pleasers who fret about what others will think of their every bite. They're relieved to be eating with others because it helps keep them "on track" (a diet word if there ever was one) and ostensibly prevents them from ordering or eating foods they believe they "shouldn't." They view others as the social control mechanism that reins in their appetites. For them, problematic food situations happen more often when they're home alone or in a room by themselves with anything edible.

The major problem with social dining is that we barely have time to consider our appetite. We end up paying attention to food in general, but not to what our bodies are saying about it. Reflection on gastronomical cues gets drowned out by chatter and groupthink, and we revert unconsciously to old habits or eat whatever everyone else is eating. Without keeping appetite signals in the forefront of awareness and having meaningful internal dialogue that will lead us to eating wisely, we too often surrender our individuality and end up with thoughts and self-talk that lead us further and further away from "normal" eating.

What's the problem when I'm eating with friends?

Just as our friends are different, so are their eating styles, habits, and attitudes about food and their bodies. Most of us have friends who generally fall into the categories of chronic dieters, "normal" eaters, or mindless eaters/overeaters. Moreover, it's not as if our friends eat the same way all the time. For the most part, "normal" eaters usually eat according to appetite, although they may occasionally overeat or undereat. Some restrictive eaters (aka chronic dieters) count calories or fat grams or eschew foods high in either. Other friends may be on the Paleo diet one week, fasting the next, and eating everything in sight the week after that. That is, some friends range from serious overeating to serious undereating, and we may never know what phase they'll be in when we make dining plans with them.

Unfortunately, this can throw off our own eating. Maybe we're thinking that they'll be eating clean, so we will too—until they order a platter of fried clams with onion rings. Or maybe we're ready to throw out the food rules and start a diet tomorrow (tomorrow being whenever Monday comes around), and our friend surprises us and orders a salad with no dressing, eats half of it, and requests a doggie bag. Unless you're grounded in your own appetite connections, what your friends eat might easily derail your best intentions.

And then there's the horrid, pervasive diet and weight talk that too often overtakes us when we're with our peers. Instead of mindfully enjoying food and discussing our lives, we end up talking about the latest diet craze, how disappointed we are at having gained or not having lost weight, our struggles with eating, and how "bad" we are. Oh, and how good we're going to be tomorrow. Rarely does discussion deepen to the sadness and despair we feel due to dysregulated eating because it's far more comfortable to talk about being "bad" than to actually feel "sad."

Moreover, we also may have friends who are binge-buddies. I had a few of them back in my wild eating days—college and my twenties—who, I'm glad to say, eat more "normally" now. Even if it was just my binge-buddy and me, the frenetic energy over food was palpable, a buzz of mutual elation about eating unhealthy treats and sweets in excessive quantities—pizza, fries, popcorn, ice cream, and birthday cakes. Anticipation made our dopamine soar, so we ignored the fact that we absolutely knew, without a doubt, that we were going to feel stomach pains galore and miserable about ourselves when the feast was over. Back then, I could down a quart of ice cream in a sitting and was strangely proud of it, though I felt sick as a dog for days afterward.

The power that food had over me in the first half of my life was total and complete, ironfisted, and it was doubly hard to resist surrendering to my eating excesses when I was with others who were similarly inclined. What a bizarre bonding experience! We were entwined in shame, the way I imagine thieves and murderers feel toward each other after they've done their dirty deed together. Not that what we did was immoral or sinful by any means, but even after all these decades have gone by, those binge parties seem simply terribly, unbearably sad and a waste of time.

With all kinds of potential eaters as co-dining friends, how does that affect our self-talk?

If we're more reactive to others' perceived or spoken judgments than we are responsive to our appetite needs, dining with friends can be crazy-making. We feel on guard and under a microscope, and our rational thoughts about eating are somewhere else. Here's some self-talk you might engage in as a dysregulated eater (DE), followed by what a "normal" eater (NE) might say in the same situation:

- (DE) I'm taking too long to decide what to eat, so I'll just order what everyone else is having.
  (NE) Even if I takes a bit longer than everyone else, I want to figure out what food will satisfy me.

- (DE) Is it really okay if I have only a bowl of soup while everyone else is ordering an entrée?
  (NE) I'm not that hungry, so I think I'll just have a bowl of soup.

- (DE) What will everyone say if I have dessert when no one else is?
  (NE) They have the best tiramisu here, so I'll have some or see if someone will share one with me.

- (DE) I'm tired of being good. I'm going to have something I *want* for a change.
  (NE) Now, what looks good on the menu?

- (DE) I'm sick of salad, but I don't want people to think that I don't care about my weight, so I'll have one anyway.
  (NE) I'm sick of salad, so let's see what else is on the menu.

- (DE) I'm so anxious about what to get—never mind eating in front of everyone—that I won't enjoy anything, so I'll have an appetizer and eat at home later.
  (NE) Good food, good friends—what could be better?

- (DE) I'm so fat, it doesn't matter what I eat.
  (NE) No matter what my size, I always want to nourish my body well.

- (DE) My friends won't care if I eat stuff that isn't good for me because they're doing the same thing.
  (NE) My friends can take care of their eating, and I'll take care of mine.

- (DE) I'll eat better tomorrow. Tonight, I just want to have fun with my friends.
  (NE) I can nourish myself and still have fun with my friends.

- (DE) I don't know how my friends have such self-control around food. I could never learn to eat like they do.
  (NE) I will honor my appetite and the needs of my body no matter what anyone else is doing.

- (DE) I'll see what other people are eating, then I'll decide what I want.
  (NE) What I eat is about what I want, not what other people are eating.

- (DE) I hate to bother the waitstaff about ingredients, so I'll just wing it and hope what I get isn't too salty.
  (NE) I'll ask the waitstaff about ingredients, so my food isn't too salty.

- (DE) I already blew it by having the fried cheese appetizer, so I might as well eat whatever I want for the rest of the meal.
  (NE) No matter what I ate, now is another moment to choose what I want.

- (DE) My friends keep looking at what I'm eating, so they must be judging me and thinking I'm eating too much.
  (NE) My friends are probably focused on their own eating.

- (DE) Everyone has stopped eating, and I'm kind of full, but I hate leaving food on my plate.
  (NE) I'm full and enjoyed my meal, so I'll get a doggie bag for what's on my plate.

- (DE) I'm going to order the lowest-calorie entrée and have a big dessert.
  (NE) I'll see if I have room for dessert and if there's anything I like on the menu.

- (DE) I could take home a doggie bag, but what I'm eating is so delicious, I just want to keep eating.
  (NE) I'm going to stop eating now and enjoy my leftovers at another time.

- (DE) All this talk about dieting and calories is making me anxious, but people will be mad if I try to change the subject.
  (NE) Ugh, diet talk. I'll throw out a more interesting topic.

- (DE) I'm so full from lunch that I don't even want dinner, but I'd look stupid not ordering anything, so I'll get an entrée and eat only a tiny bit of it.
  (NE) Who cares what other people think about what or how much I'm eating?

- (DE) I'll just eat a lot now for brunch and not eat again until tomorrow.
  (NE) I'll eat until I'm satiated and then stop.

How can I keep self-talk sane when food and family collide?

Yup, I can hear the groans. Eating with family—our family of origin or procreation—can be enormously stressful for a dysregulated eater. All the badgering, nudging, digs, eyebrow raising, harping, and words left unsaid can be off-putting and annoying even for "normal" eaters who feel generally accepting of how they feed themselves. But for dysregulated eaters, how family members view and deal with you, your size, and your choices can be the straw that breaks the camel's back.

It *can* be, but it need *not* be. Self-talk is the determining factor—not weight, childhood experiences, personality-disordered relatives, or stress—in how we respond to our families around food. Of course, self-talk is based on beliefs, so it helps to have functional cognitions upon which to base positive self-talk. It's important to remind yourself that you can handle any eating or weight comments by relatives who mean well but think they know better than you do regarding what and how to feed your body. To learn more about creating healthy, rational beliefs, take a look at my book *The Rules of "Normal" Eating*.

Obvious conflicts with family members include comments to you or others about eating or weight, trying overtly or covertly to steer you away or push you toward certain foods, and using body language (grimaces, eye rolls, dagger looks, sighs) that imply that there's something wrong with your size or what you're putting into your mouth.

Most dysregulated eaters grew up with some kind of eating dysfunction going on in their family. That's how they got to be troubled eaters. Mom, struggling to stay on a diet, wanted you to eat as she did because she feared your weight would inch up like hers has. Dad was always pressuring you to go out and run with him to keep trim. Grandma got insulted when you refused second helpings of her homemade dishes and insisted you take home leftovers. Grandpa made blatant remarks about you eating too much, or your brother teased you about being too fat for anyone to date.

Or your family had no rules about what foods were nourishing, and most of your meals came from a jar, can, package, or fast-food restaurant. Meals at home were eaten in front of the TV, or rather than soften the mood and eat by candlelight, family members ate by computer light. You never discussed nutrition and portion size, and since everyone turned to food for fun and to de-stress, heck, you did, too.

Family attitudes about eating and weight come from a variety of sources. Remember that your family members also engaged in self-talk and conversation, some positive and some negative, about food and what people ought to weigh. It's not as if they awakened every morning and thought about how they could indoctrinate you with their ideas on the subject. But listening to and watching our parents and relatives is how we learn when we don't even know we're learning. Most of the time they thought what they thought because they didn't know any better and said what they said because they loved and wanted the best for you. Really, there was no plot to put the kibosh on your relationship with food.

If you were fortunate, as you've matured, so have your family members, and they've started to mind their own business and quit focusing on what you eat and weigh. Sadly, in my experience, many parents (and other relatives) continue to bombard their adult children with unwanted advice about how to feed themselves and what size they should be, much to the appropriate consternation of these adult children. Worse, everything your family members have said to and about you since you were a child has become lodged in your head, and you've confused it with truth.

These perceptions can only be repaired consciously. For example, when I was a teenager standing in front of the mirror, my mother would often sigh and admonish, "You should see what you look like from the back," referring to my beehive hairdo or short skirt. So what do you think would be my last instruction to myself before leaving the house each day now if I didn't work to block it out of consciousness? Of course, I'd be telling myself that I dare not leave without checking to see what I look like from the back. So much for well-meant motherly advice.

In order to counter our childhood and cultural brainwashing, let's do what we did with friends and take a look at the unhealthy self-talk (U for unhealthy) versus healthy self-talk (H for healthy) that you might have with family around food and weight:

- (U) My parents are going to be so upset that I've put on weight since the last time I saw them.
  (H) If my parents make comments about my eating or weight, I'll chalk it up to their worrying about me and respectfully decline to engage.

- (U) I'm so anxious around my family that my eating will be worse than ever.
  (H) I'll take breaks from the family whenever I need to, do deep breathing, and visualize myself being calm around them.

- (U) My sister will want to talk about her newest diet, and I'll just have to listen to her even though I'm sick of diet talk.
  (H) I'll change the subject if my sister brings up what she's eating and not eating.

- (U) I'd better not eat much when I'm with my family so they won't think I don't care about my weight.
  (H) I'll eat according to my appetite and not worry about what anyone's thinking.

- (U) I know I'm going to be bad around food, and I can't help it.
  (H) I'll listen to my appetite and eat accordingly.

- (U) My cousin will be upset if we don't go out together and eat till we're stuffed.
  (H) I'll tell my cousin I don't stuff myself with food anymore.

- (U) I can't say no to all the special treats that are around when I'm with family.

  (H) I will eat what and however much I consciously want and be proud of myself.

- (U) If we go to my favorite restaurant, I'll just start a diet tomorrow.

  (H) If we go to my favorite restaurant, I'll be mindful of my choices like always.

- (U) I can't say no to eating dessert in front of the TV with my family, though I know that's a setup for me to overeat.

  (H) I don't like eating in front of the TV very much, so I'll decline dessert or, if I want it, I'll have it later when I can eat more mindfully.

- (U) I'll be good eating at dinner and sneak food up to my room the way I used to if there's some food I don't want to miss.

  (H) I'll eat foods I want and enjoy them in front of my family.

Imagine saying all that positive, healthy self-talk when you're with your family.

Visualize how free and proud you'll feel. Think of each word and sentence as actively massaging your brain and transforming your thinking and behavior in a positive direction. Of course, you might be telling yourself right now, "I can't possibly say all those things. I'd be way too uncomfortable. I don't want to rock the boat." Instead, why not say, "I can do this. As an adult, I'll think and say what I want to take care of myself when I'm with family—and love how I feel when I do it!" I promise, your self-talk will improve a little bit more every time you practice it around family. Each time you'll do even better than the last time. Eventually, this will be how you behave and speak around your relatives. Won't that be a kick?

> ### Thoughts to Munch On
>
> • What has been your most difficult social eating situation?
> • How do you wish to feel about social eating?
> • What habits help you relax in social eating situations?

What's the best recipe for food problems and romance?

Dating is stressful enough without tossing food into the picture. The last thing you want to do is add more agita to dating by worrying about eating with someone on whom you want to make a good impression and who makes your heart sing. The truth is that most people are anxious about dating, and some will even admit it. If you're a bit nervous, that's normal. Just make sure your self-patter relaxes you and doesn't ratchet up your fears. Think about how you want to feel dining wherever you'll be (at your place, his, hers, or at a restaurant), and adjust your self-talk accordingly.

If you're used to worrying about your size or weight, you'll have to put those thoughts aside to stay in a relaxed mood. Many high-weight people fear that a date won't like them because of their size. They get so caught up in nightmares of rejection that it's hard to be themselves. It's true that someone you go out with may not care for you because of your size—or for many other reasons. You can't control his or her or anyone's reaction to you, but you can control your thoughts.

Here are some ways to swap out anxious, negative self-talk (U for unhealthy) for calming, positive words of self-love, pride, compassion, and respect (H for healthy):

- (U) I'm twenty pounds heavier than in my dating site photo. He'll be so disappointed.

  (H) I have a great deal to offer in a relationship, and that's what I'll show him.

- (U) I'm so nervous when I go out with someone, I'm sure I'll overeat.

  (H) I'm calm and attractive and interesting, and I'll do fine with food.

- (U) I hate going to new restaurants with women I don't know. I take forever trying to figure out what to order, and they think I'm weird.

  (H) I'll check out the menu online in advance and get an idea of what to eat.

- (U) At my size, she'll be watching every mouthful I take, so how can I eat and relax?

  (H) I'm allowed to enjoy food and nourish my body, so I'll focus on mindful eating and not on what she might think of me.

- (U) What if he makes a huge dinner for me and I eat it all? What will he think?

  (H) If I eat a lot, he'll think he's a great cook! I'll stay focused on my appetite and not worry about anything else.

- (U) I'll tell her about my dieting history so she'll at least know I've tried to lose weight.

  (H) My diet history is my business. I don't have to prove anything to her.

- (U) I see her looking at thinner people, and I bet she'd rather be with them.
  (H) She's with me, and I'm not going to undermine my happiness with anxiety.

- (U) I know I have good qualities, but they don't matter at my size.
  (H) I have plenty of wonderful qualities and am lovable at any size.

- (U) I want to have sex with her, but I'm ashamed of my body.
  (H) If she's interested in having sex with me, I'll go for it with gusto.

- (U) I'd like to see him again but won't because he'll only decide I'm too fat for him in the long run.
  (H) If he wants a second date, I'll go and assume the best until I know differently.

At the other end of the continuum from dating, having a partner when you're a dysregulated eater is often no picnic. He nags you because he loves you. She tries to cook only healthy dishes fearing that left to your own devices with food you'll have a second heart attack. Once more, this is a time to remember that you're with someone who loves and cares greatly about you. If you're not, either get couples therapy to improve the relationship or get out of it. Life's too short to put up with less when you deserve more. And, in too many cases, being mistreated by your partner may be one of the reasons you eat emotionally.

Many different dynamics, both subtle and obvious, occur between two people in a relationship, and these can impact how you talk about weight and act around food for better or for worse. Sometimes you contribute to these interpersonal problems because you give double messages to your partner. You might ask him to cook only nutritious foods and then sneak snacks behind his back. Or you might complain when she insists on keeping sugary treats in the house for herself and the kids but finish them off yourself.

You both might have eating problems and unconsciously know that one person eating more "normally" will ruin all the fun of "being bad" together. You or your partner (or both of you) may be codependent, focusing on the other person's problem rather than on your own difficulties with food or other addictions. Your spouse may fear that if you lose weight, you'll leave her. Your partner may wish you were thinner because he wants to boost his ego and show the world that he can get a culturally approved hottie. You may refuse to have sex with your spouse because you feel too fat to be seen naked.

Warning: Your relationship may be collateral damage if you become healthier around food because of the major changes that will occur in your self-esteem and sense of empowerment. There's no guarantee that you both will grow, mature, and change, but that's no reason not to put your all into healing from food problems. If you feel better about yourself, you may resent the (often long-standing) mistreatment by your partner over food and other issues. Sometimes your partner will be willing and able to grow healthier with you, and the relationship will blossom. Other times, he or she won't put in the effort or simply can't do the transformative work that's necessary for you two to stay together. This is not an unusual occurrence in recovery and may lead to ending the relationship.

Nevertheless, there is self-talk that will keep your eating problems going (U for unhealthy) and self-talk that will help you become healthier (H for healthy) about food and your body in a long-term relationship:

- (U) I don't blame him for not wanting to touch or have sex with me at my size. I wouldn't want to either.
  (H) I deserve to be touched no matter what my size is. High-weight people cuddle and have sex, so why shouldn't I?

- (U) I don't blame her for being ashamed of going out socially with me and introducing me to people because of my weight.
  (H) High-weight people have the right to be valued and admired and to go wherever they want to go.

- (U) I don't have the willpower to not eat certain foods, so I'll ask him to stop me from eating them.
  (H) I'm responsible for what I eat and don't eat, and I'll only resent him if I give him power over my feeding habits.

- (U) I'm afraid that if I lose weight, I'll want to end my unhappy marriage.
  (H) If my relationship makes me unhappy, I will get help to see if we can save it and, if not, I will leave it.

- (U) If he becomes a "normal" eater and I don't, I'll be left behind.
  (H) I want to be a "normal" eater for many great reasons, including being with him.

- (U) I don't like when he teases me about my weight, but I can't blame him.
  (H) I don't deserve to be teased about my weight, and I'll tell him how it hurts and that I want him to stop doing it.

- (U) I kind of like how she worries about my weight because then I know she cares about me. If I don't have an eating problem, how will she show her caring?
  (H) I don't need to have problems for her to care about me. I can tell her other ways she can show caring.

- (U) If I lose weight, I'll cheat on her like I did the last time I slimmed down.
  (H) I can lose weight and be faithful to her. I may need to see a therapist to help me do that.

- (U) I love going out to dinner with him because I hate cooking, but I'm scared of all the menu temptations in restaurants.
  (H) I want to eat well and can't do that right now by going out to dinner so often, so I'll speak to him about us cooking at home together more.

- (U) I don't like having sex anymore, and staying at a high weight is a good way to make sure that doesn't happen.
  (H) I'll have an open discussion with him about our sexual relationship, and we'll work something out that meets both of our needs.

I hope you can see how positive self-talk empowers you and helps individuation—becoming your own person—within a couple. The smart self-talk above develops from being honest with and knowing yourself. Just getting to your truth is a big step in recovery, because growing emotionally healthier is not only about improving your relationship with food; it's about learning who you want to be and then moving forward to become that person.

Can I really be a "normal" eater at a buffet or party?

Even dysregulated eaters who manage to do fairly well nourishing themselves at home, at restaurants, and eating with friends, family, dates, or mates, often panic when an invitation to a food-filled event comes along. Immediately, their default negative self-talk takes over. "I don't want to go . . . I'll gain ten pounds . . . It'll blow how well I've been doing . . . Just thinking of all that food makes me anxious . . . Ugh, I begged off last year, so I guess I'll have to go this time."

This is what it's come to: quaking at the thought of a spread of delicious food that you didn't lift a finger to shop for, didn't slave to cook, don't have to serve to others, and won't be called upon to clean up after eating. "Normal" eaters call this heaven, while you call it hell. In fact, most dysregulated eaters feel both dread and desire at contemplating buffets or parties. You're excited about the variety of foods you'll get to choose from, but you're also terrified by how much you may eat. Most of your worry is driven by nightmarish memories of previous feeding frenzies when copious amounts and varieties of food were all too readily available. You can almost taste your dread.

Here are some great strategies for eating at a party or buffet:

- Sit or stand facing away from the food.
- Find out beforehand what food will be served so that you can consider your options.
- At a buffet, peruse the food *before* taking any, and make mental notes about what you would most enjoy eating.
- Take only small amounts of foods you love, and remember that what you're seeing may be the first of several courses.
- Don't go for seconds unless you're eating only a couple of selections, and even then, keep seconds small.

- Tune out the chatter of other guests about what they're eating or not eating and especially their fears of feeling pressured to eat everything in sight.
- Don't rush up to the food line when you arrive or as soon as it's put out; instead, give yourself time to take in your surroundings, talk with people, and relax.
- Focus on conversation, not food, and don't talk when you're eating or eat when you're talking.
- Chew food well and let it sit on your tongue so that your taste buds can do their job of registering taste, satiation, and fullness.
- Eat as slowly as you can by pausing after every mouthful.
- Use deep breathing to keep yourself relaxed.

Along with these strategies, you'll reduce food reactivity by keeping self-talk goal oriented, positive, and rational to tamp down anxiety and generate calm and confidence. It's not as hard as you may think. Here's how you might approach a food-laden event by avoiding unhealthy self-talk (U for unhealthy) and turning up the volume on a healthy soundtrack (H for healthy) to accompany your meal:

- (U) I'm really anxious about what I'll eat. I have a terrible track record eating at parties.

  (H) I'll put full attention on my appetite to guide me, be mindful of my choices, and eat just the right amount of food for me.

- (U) I'll starve myself all day so I can eat whatever I want tonight.

  (H) I'll keep myself nourished during the day so I won't overeat tonight.

- (U) Every time I look at all those foods I love, I just know I'll overeat.
  (H) I'll eat mindfully and slowly, chew my food thoroughly, and let food sit on my tongue to savor it.

- (U) I need to get to the food table right away to make sure I get the foods I want.
  (H) I'll let others get their food and know there'll still be plenty left for me, because I don't make good food decisions when I feel pressured.

- (U) There's so much yummy food to choose from; I want to taste everything.
  (H) I can't possibly taste every food, so I'll go only for my favorites and leave the rest.

- (U) I'll have a second helping of the yummy cheese and crackers and eat less during the rest of the meal.
  (H) The cheese and crackers were delicious, but no more for now because I want to save room for other foods I like.

- (U) I'm already full, but I can't say no to dessert.
  (H) I'll wait a bit and see if I have room for dessert. If not, no big deal.

- (U) I've been really good all week waiting to eat at this party, and it's not fair that I shouldn't get to eat everything I want.
  (H) I'll base my food decisions not on fairness, but on appetite, health, and pride.

- (U) I don't care how I'll feel later. I want more food now, so I'll just cut back eating next week or go to the gym more often.
  (H) I care a lot about how I'll feel later, so I'll enjoy what I can and eat until I'm satisfied then stop

- (U) I can't believe I ate so much. I'm so stupid. I knew this would happen. I'll never be a "normal" eater.
  (H) Though I ate more than I hoped I would, I'm not a bad person and forgive myself for overeating.

Imagine what you would feel like saying all these positive things to yourself.

Better yet, imagine how you would eat. Remember that what you tell your brain is like programming a computer. What you say to it—your brain or the computer—is what it will do. Honestly, once you know what to say, it's as easy to say something wise as something unwise. Remember, too, that every time you speak positively and compassionately to yourself, you're cementing a habit and a practice that you'll enjoy for the rest of your life.

In chapter 8, you'll learn about the best motivator of them all and how to make it work to improve your eating and general self-caring. It's an emotion that dysregulated eaters are not accustomed to experiencing, but one that brings such widespread reward it's irresistible. It's the perfect icing on the cake in a book about self-talk.

● ● ●

Case Study: **Quinn**

Quinn, a sixty-two-year-old woman, always looks picture perfect, from her expensive haircut to her designer shoes to her flawless skin. She came to see me because her bulimia, which she'd had thirty years prior, had recently returned. Her longtime partner had left her for a younger woman, and Quinn missed her "beyond words." She felt thrown back into a social scene similar to what she steered clear of in her younger days, and she felt isolated and "forlorn" if she didn't partake of it. So she didn't go out much and, instead, picked at food all day long and sometimes even rose in the middle of the night to raid the refrigerator.

An introverted artist and local minor celebrity, she had the good fortune to make her own work and eating schedule and avoid social eating and drinking activities by using the excuse that she was finishing a project. The truth was that she'd been able to manage her food problems only by rigidly structuring her life and her eating. She felt that she couldn't eat well when she was with other people because she became distracted from her own appetite by what they were eating and talking about.

Her mother also was an artist, and Quinn wondered if she was mildly agoraphobic. Because of this, her father took Quinn out to social gatherings as his "date." In fact, she said, though socializing was always stressful for her, her father loved to show off his beautiful, talented, model-thin daughter. She was never relaxed eating at parties or in the homes of others, feeling pressured to eat to please the host or hostess yet sensing her father's watchful eye on what and how much food was on her plate.

Her initial self-talk reflected her fears:

- I'm out of control when I'm not eating alone or in my own home.

- I can't connect to my appetite and please others when I'm eating.
- If I eat what I want, I won't be thin and attractive.
- If I eat out, I'll get fat.
- Eating at home makes me feel safe and secure but very lonely.

Quinn's resumption of bulimic behavior was her way to avoid experiencing the tremendous grief and void of losing her longtime partner as well as coming to terms with aging. She'd never resolved her social anxieties that had begun in childhood. Now going out and being alone both seemed like untenable choices. She agreed that food and weight were a perfect red herring when she didn't wish to experience more painful, personal emotions and that controlling food intake or weight became a substitute for managing anxieties in the larger world.

The self-talk Quinn chose to use going forward was meant to soothe the anxieties that drove her to both binge and purge and to help her feel more relaxed with people. Here is some of it:

- I manage my appetite, and I am the only one to hear its cues.
- No matter where I eat or with whom, I am solely in charge of feeding myself.
- I can relax and enjoy people.
- I find pleasure in being alone, with people, with food, or without food.
- My beauty comes from within not without, and that gives me freedom.

Quinn picked an arbitrary date to give up purging and, after a few relapses from which she learned a great deal, quit the habit over the span of about six months. Surprisingly, she gave herself permission to gain a few pounds until her grief subsided, which made it easier to quit purging and also to attend social events where there would be food—a healthy solution. She widened her dining experiences with her social circle gradually, first dining out with only one other person, then expanding to a few close friends, and finally going to an occasional party. She still sometimes couldn't eat at parties or she overate, but she was far less anxious about social eating. When she left therapy, she was still grappling with aging and appearance issues and how to be an introvert in a world of extroverts, but she'd left behind the excessive pressure she felt to be thin and beautiful.

CHAPTER 8

Think Proud, Talk Proud, Act Proud, Be Proud

(Nothing Tastes Better than Pride!)

You'd think it would be a no-brainer that everyone would want to feel proud of themselves all the time, or at least as often as possible. Why wouldn't they? It's a glorious, heady, awesome high like no other. Plus, unlike so many aspects of life, you have the option to control whether and how often you feel proud. You turn it on, you turn it off—simply by what you think and do. Really, it's that easy.

Oddly enough, although it's a joyous experience, many folks are wary or scornful of feeling proud. This in itself is a major reason they remain stuck in an eating rut, ashamed of their behaviors. After all, what's the opposite of pride? Shame, of course. It's amazing how many clients live in shame because it's familiar and run from pride because they have an entirely wrongheaded concept of what it means to enjoy it. They're overwhelmed with shame for being out of control around food, and it oozes out of them and smears every aspect of their lives. Yet, when I explain that they're needlessly suffering and struggling through shame-based lives, they cling to their self-hate and disdain as if it were a prized possession—then make me work to pry it away from them. Why is that, do you think?

Decades ago, I had a client whose father used to beat her and her younger brother with a serrated-edged saw palmetto branch when she was a child. Dad, a military man, was a violent alcoholic and wife-beater, and my client suffered terribly growing up under his roof. Raised in this shame-based family—all alcoholic and abusive families are, because of the shame generated by these behaviors—she turned into a shame-based woman who married an abusive man. In our sessions, she shared her regret and remorse that she hadn't protected her younger brother from her father's rages and her own daughter from her husband's physical and emotional abuse. Throw in her extramarital affair, excessive drinking, high weight, and love of high-fat, high-sugar foods, and she'd felt mired in shame most of the time. Worse, she couldn't imagine feeling any other way.

When I asked what she felt proud of, she started to cry. She couldn't even say the words "pride" or "proud" because her father would take a branch to her bottom if he heard her boasting about her accomplishments or drawing any kind of positive attention to herself. For years in therapy, we settled on her calling pride "the P word" until she could say the entire word aloud to me and feel, well, proud of doing so. It was a place to start.

What's wrong with feeling shame?

Shame has an evolutionary purpose: It functions as an alert that you may have thought or done something that fails to meet your own or your community's standards and gives you pause that your thoughts or actions may not be in your best interest or the interests of those around you. (for more information on shame, read my chapter on it in my *Food and Feelings Workbook*). There's nothing wrong with feeling a ping of shame to tell you that you haven't lived up to your standards or those of the larger world. However, there's everything wrong with living a shame-based life and never feeling good enough.

Shame is beyond embarrassment (aka shame light) and disappointment in yourself. It's a sucker punch to your gut that says you've failed, ought to have done better, shouldn't have bothered, aren't worth it, didn't try hard enough, and maybe are such a terrible person the world would be better off without you. Shame insists that you're defective and, worse, unfixable. As ongoing fuel for motivation, it's a failure, a flop, the sham that will, with 100 percent certainty, keep you under its thumb, kill your spirit, and never let you live your dreams.

And then there's shame's cousin—disgust—which is like shame on steroids. As a dysregulated eater, you may put on weight until you're disgusted with and can't stand the sight of yourself. So you vow to slim down and start doing the "right" things—making nutritious food choices, exercising regularly, following the rules of "normal" eating, and staying conscious about food without obsessing about it. Gradually, as you move toward these goals, the shame and disgust start to lift and you feel sweet relief. Fearing the return of shame and disgust, you remain motivated and on a roll for a few weeks or several months or even years until slowly, little by little, you stop engaging in healthy behaviors—you eat past full a few times, skip the gym for a week, have a binge or ten, and resume mindless snacking. Soon you're back in the whole shame-and-disgust cycle all over again.

What's missing is an understanding of how shame will boomerang you right back to square one every time. The problem is that you've become accustomed to using shame to keep yourself pumped and disgust to keep yourself moving toward your eating goals. You think, "If I can just keep eating right / going to the gym / walking each day / cooking healthy meals, I won't feel shame. If I always stay one step ahead of it, I can keep it at bay." These emotions may work to jump-start your best intentions—in fact, they often do—but once you begin doing what's beneficial on a regular basis, you stop feeling shame and disgust and need another emotion to keep you moving in a positive direction.

Here's the underlying problem with these dynamics. Hoping they'll prevent you from stepping out of line or falling off the wagon, you employ shame and disgust to work motivational wonders they were not meant to work. Your strategy for avoiding failure is policing yourself and doing the "right" things to lose weight, eating nutritiously and staying active. Yet, there are so many unmet cravings and desires nipping at your heels that you sometimes falter and give in to them. Then, due to the intense pressure to outrun shame and "be good" twenty-four seven, sooner or later you start to resent what you believe you *must* do. Between your unmet cravings and desires and the plethora of shoulds, you think, "Enough already. I'm exhausted, and I've got nothing left to give. I can't do this anymore."

You miss one yoga class and then another, start picking at the treats in the break room, quit buying healthy fruits and vegetables, and resume swinging by Wendy's after work. You become lax and slip backward, watching all your hard work unravel and disappear. Fear of shame has stopped working like it used to. It's morphed into a low-level background tension eating away at your self-esteem and reminding you of the better (slimmer) person you were, the person you aren't now and maybe were never meant to be.

Or you use others to help you shame yourself. Initially, you look to people to remind you what a wonderful job you're doing taking care of yourself: cooking wholesome meals at home, never missing a morning constitutional with your walking group, and learning to meditate to reduce stress-eating. You receive tons of accolades for the changes you've made, especially if you've begun to shed pounds. You gobble up the praise because it's another way to keep away the shame. You think, "If others tell me I'm doing great, it must be true. I guess I don't need to be ashamed anymore."

But gradually the praise fades as how you look and the positive behaviors you're engaging in become the new normal and your weight loss slows down or plateaus. Your behavior is no longer newly transformational or praiseworthy. What happens when the compliments and attention drop off? How do you feel when the cheerleading ends? There goes your incentive. What, then, is your motivation for doing what's beneficial for yourself?

The truth is that self-shame and seeking approval from others is a red herring. It's time to admit the truth. This is a major step in recovery from dysregulated eating. Repeat after me: "Shaming myself about my eating and weight and doing the 'right' things in order to get praise from others (or avoid their scorn) for healthy eating and regular exercise does not work long-term." Keep repeating this sentence until it has sunk in and you embrace the truth.

In order to not boomerang back after losing weight, you need sustained motivation and incentives that keep on ticking. The idea isn't to win someone's approval or to reach goals so that you can then relax. You want to keep at it because you are worth it, want to be healthy, don't wish to die prematurely, and feel substantially better physically and emotionally when you act in self-nurturing ways. In short, you prefer the results of taking care of yourself to the results of acting self-destructively.

If you're stuck in this self-disgust/rebellion cycle described above, it's time to break it, to drop it like a hot potato. Refuse to hate your body, refuse to feel disgust when you look in the mirror, refuse to ever get on a scale again. Eliminate shoulds from your thinking and begin framing moving forward as what you desire from your heart. Live in a world that is full of wishes rather than shoulds. And cultivate pride.

Why is pride so important?

What, you might wonder, does pride have to do with self-talk? The answer is *everything*. Most dysregulated eaters' self-talk, especially of the unconscious variety, is negative and reeks of shame. It admonishes us about what we must never do in order to be acceptable human beings, blames us for our never-ending deficits, denigrates our value to ourselves and others, and is like self-flagellation with the palmetto branch my client's father used to beat her and her brother.

Most, if not all, dysregulated eaters' self-talk is shame-based. I know because they share it with me during therapy sessions, and it's everything I used to say to my former dysregulated-eating self. It's meant to make you feel defective and to motivate you to get your loser act together and, for Pete's sake, do what's "right" for yourself for a change. Shame-based self-talk is full of contempt, disgust, frustration, self-pity, and condescension, and it sounds like it's coming from a know-it-all bully. It makes no sense to think we could use contemptuous put-downs to do something that's supposed to be positive for ourselves.

We hope that by saying negative things about and to ourselves in an I-mean-it-this-time-Buster sort of way, we'll end up with a successful result. Sadly, that rarely happens, or, if it does, it fails to last for long. It's not because we're not trying hard enough or there's something defective about us. The reason it doesn't get us where we want to go—or, more precisely, keep us there—is that it does the opposite of inspiring and sustaining transformation. It only points out where we've failed, how low we've stooped, and how far we need to climb to crawl out of the gutter of shame that we can't seem to stay out of for long.

Sadly, dysregulated eaters are taught (at least in this culture) that being hard on themselves is the best change agent. I hope I've convinced you that it's nothing of the sort. You can't hate yourself thin or healthy or fit, you can't dwell on ugliness and produce beauty, and you can't keep putting yourself down to raise yourself up. So if shame isn't the way to stop self-destructive behavior and build a life based on constructive, wise thought and smart action, what's its replacement?

It's pride, of course. I'm not talking about feeling proud *after* you've accomplished something but about feeling ongoing delight in and satisfaction with yourself *as* you're trying to do it. It's easy to feel happiness *after* your gym workout, *after* the trip to the grocery store to fill your cart with fresh fruits and vegetables, *after* having spent twenty minutes making yourself a tasty meal at home that makes you feel nourished. The point is to feel proud of yourself *because* you're doing it. The idea is to keep pride pumping from the moment you set an intention through all the moments of follow-through, to savoring the joy of a mission accomplished. And to look forward to repeating this process again and again.

Remember how your parents or teachers used to tell you that it's the effort that counts? That effort is what I'm calling pride. The fact that you're struggling to do something beautiful for yourself even though it's a challenge. The fact that you think well enough of yourself to try and keep trying. It's the rain on the flowers, not their blossoms and the locker room pep talks whether the team wins or not. This is pride, and if you infuse your self-talk with it, it will revolutionize your life, especially your ability to take care of yourself.

Are there different kinds of motivation?

I've talked about how shame is a spirit-killing, failure-prone, dead-end motivator. Now it's time to talk about how pride can successfully replace it. To do that, I need to explain and differentiate two kinds of motivation: external and internal. External motivators are based on factors outside of ourselves—the approval of others or fear of punishment if we don't succeed. They're the prizes we hope or expect to win when we reach our goals, the brass ring or pot of gold at the end of the rainbow. External motivators work like this: We do X and anticipate getting Y for it. Then we walk around thrilled that we finally have Y (praise from Dad, a date with someone we've been crushing on, all As, or oohs and aahs from our best buds).

All's well if you try and succeed. It means you've outwitted failure and shame once again (whew!) and confirms that your stock is high because you've received validation that you're as good as you think you are or hoped you'd be. But with this kind of thinking comes the unconscious recognition of the underbelly of success: thinking that you could or might have failed. It's scary to know that no matter what accolades you receive or prizes you win, that next time you may not be so lucky—and then what?

Remember, in chapter 2 you learned the shame-based words that fall under the umbrella of external motivators: "should," "shouldn't," "ought to," "must," "have to," and "am supposed to." And, of course, my Nana's favorite, "dasn't." Feel that finger shaking at you, scolding you to be "good" not "bad" and the look of disdain that accompanies it? How great does that feel? That's the shaming experience when you use external motivation.

Internal motivation, on the other hand, is about how you feel doing something because it's the best thing to do for yourself, speaks to the kind of person you wish to be, and underscores your goal of caring well for yourself and others. With internal motivation, we shine for no one but ourselves. If our glow warms others and brightens their lives, all the better. Sure, it feels wonderful to get compliments and praise, but they're just icing on the cake. What feels like nothing else in the world is the pride of doing something that expresses who you are or want to be. Forget the applause. It's knowing that you deserve to be on stage whether you're up there or not. It's enjoying dancing when no one is watching, a unique expression of your ongoing, unwavering devotion to be your best self *for yourself*.

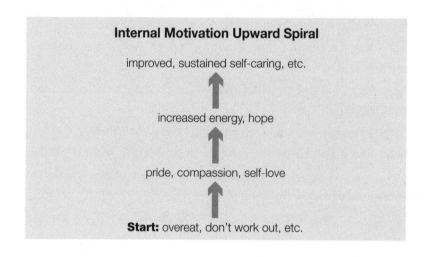

With internal motivation, you care about outcomes and look forward to success, but that's only part of why you do something. I write books because I love writing. I've been doing it since adolescence because I adore the process. It thrills me, even when I'm doing a mediocre job of expressing myself or when I'm frustrated. Do I hope when I have a book idea that I'll find a publisher? Of course. Do I want the book to sell well? By all means. But even if my publishing wishes or dreams don't come true, nothing can take away the joy of birthing a heartfelt desire into the world, riding a high while writing, or the satisfaction I feel spending time getting out the message about something I passionately care about.

Here's how shame and pride work as motivators. You tell your-self, "Get off your duff, you worthless sack of fat, and go to the gym. Your membership is almost expired, and you've been, what, three times? Pathetic." How can you not feel crummy, guilty, and disappointed in your pathetic lump of a self? "All right," you tell yourself half-heartedly, "I'll go to the damned gym."

But if you're so pathetic and worthless, what's the point? Your words and attitude suck the energy right out of you, and suddenly you're exhausted and dispirited. All you want to do is burrow into a batch of chocolate chip cookie dough and stay there licking your lips forever. Consider this: You're telling yourself you're all these terrible things, including that you're practically worthless, so why on earth would you be motivated to do something positive for such a worthless self?

Alternately, you could tell yourself, "You are worthwhile and lov-able, even if you haven't been to the gym in a long while. Whether you go or not, you deserve the best in life and are a fine and decent human being. As such, you'll feel better about yourself if you go to the gym, not only because your body will thank you but also because you'll be doing something to take care of your fabulous self. You want that for yourself, so go on and get your track shoes on and find your water bottle." After saying these words, you feel uplifted and not so subhuman. The words and tone energize you, as if it matters more than anything that you take this one step forward. So you take it.

Internal motivators are the words want, wish, would like, prefer, and desire. They're whole-hearted and hold no judgment. They're replete with passion and full-steam-ahead promise. You don't need any other words to keep you motivated.

Pride is just about as internal as you can get because it con-nects you with your deepest, fullest, most loving self and longings.

Shame, on the other hand, springs from your fears, the pain you've experienced, and your terror of ever again returning to such suffering. If I were to give shame an image, it would be a swamp with grabby things pulling you down into sludgy water. Pride, on the other hand, would be the sun's rays reaching out to give you a well-deserved hug. It would be like a smile living inside you growing bigger and brighter. Thinking of it that way, which kind of motivation would you choose?

Thoughts to Munch On

- Do you carry a great deal of shame that doesn't belong to you from your childhood?
- Are you ready to feel worthy, deserving, and proud of yourself?
- What words could you use to boost your pride?

Use pride to stay motivated.

Pride really is a wonder of a power-packed emotion. It's like one of those all-purpose kitchen gadgets or camping tools that can do just about anything you need done, or a miracle drug that heals all diseases. Need a perk-me-up? Count the reasons you value yourself or why you're proud to be you. Fell off the wagon? Focus on how you climbed right back on this time, more quickly than ever before. Worried you'll never have a positive relationship with food and your body? Notice how far you've come and what you've accomplished so far (exercising regularly, cutting back on portion size most of the time, not cleaning your plate every meal). Pride is good for whatever ails you.

My favorite use of pride is in making decisions, with the goal of feeling proud of yourself as often as possible. When we make choices that are doing what's best for ourselves and live up to our ideals, we feel proud. When we fail to live up to them, we feel ashamed. Why wouldn't you want to live up to them and feel proud every time you have a chance?

Of course, some decisions are clear-cut, and others are more nuanced. Examples of obvious wise choices include seeing someone drop his or her wallet and picking it up and returning it to his or her, calming yourself down by counting to ten before reacting to your toddler who's tracked mud onto your new white rug, or not finishing the bag of chips while watching TV because you already were full from dinner when you started eating them. Clear-cut decisions are ones that pretty much everyone would agree are wise to do: We don't steal someone's possessions, we work hard not to lose our temper with toddlers, and we resist hurting ourselves by eating past full.

If only all the do's and don'ts of life were so clearly delineated— like what to do about eating a candy bar? You can't say that having a candy bar is always the wrong choice. If it's an occasional treat that's eaten mindfully, it could be just the thing to hit the spot. However, if you eat three candy bars every day, there's a good chance you're harming your health. Likewise, if you eat one so fast you don't even taste it or feel so guilty afterward that you believe the day is blown eating-wise and therefore eat another one.

You can see that whether or not to eat the candy bar is situationally based. Relevance and context matter a great deal. Eating a candy bar when you're angry to stuff down feelings would lead to shame if your goal is to be healthier. Eating a candy bar slowly, attentively, and joyfully as a sweet indulgence would make you proud because eating delicious food mindfully is part of self-caring.

Declining to take a friend to the airport could make you either proud or ashamed, depending on the circumstances, as would putting in overtime at work or telling a friend how you really feel about them. Though you may have been taught so, most of life isn't about being or doing "right" or "wrong" in a vacuum. If you've been schooled in that kind of simplistic, childlike thinking (because that's what your parents did to get through life) and still use it, you'll need to learn to view and solve problems in a far more nuanced, complex, mature way through developing critical-thinking skills. To do so, see chapter 7, Problem Solving and Critical Thinking, in my book *Outsmarting Overeating*.

Often we're not sure what to do when making a decision and need to consider how we're going to feel in the long term. However, more often than not, the choice of pride versus shame in a situation is pretty straightforward. We know how we're going to feel most of the time if we do this or that, especially in the realm of eating, fitness, or self-caring. The key is to be aware when you're making a decision that making choice A will cause you to feel ashamed and making choice B will enhance your self-pride. You can crawl more deeply into your shame cave, or you can lift yourself out of it by acknowledging that you're not perfect and neither is anyone else and that it's your job to raise your own spirits and do right by yourself.

Thoughts to Munch On

- What would life be like if you mostly made decisions that made you proud?

- How would that feel compared to how you make decisions and feel now?

- Start a pride journal that includes all the small, proud moments you experience every day, then stop and feel proud that you're moving toward emotional health.

Say you've just been dumped by your lover or lost your job, had a huge blowup that was your fault with your parents/children/spouse/partner, and hate that you spent all weekend on your couch eating everything in your kitchen cabinets. All you can think about is what a mess you've made of your life, and so you make it worse by getting down on yourself—which, of course, makes you feel more ashamed and more inclined to eat mindlessly.

This is a perfect choice point, a time to say to yourself, "Okay, that was yesterday, and this is today. And right now I'm going to lead with self-compassion, change course, and do something that will make me proud of myself." You don't need to engage in some grand gesture like going to a spa for a week or writing a check to your local animal shelter that will wipe out your savings account. The point is to act in small ways that you know are healthy and make you feel better.

Every moment counts equally with every other moment. Be careful not to give more weight to what you perceive yourself doing "poorly" than to what you perceive yourself doing "well." The decision point when you say no to that second helping of apple pie is as important as the one when you cave and eat three pieces.

Don't just do what makes you proud but enjoy feeling awesome.

Ready for more ways to use pride as the ultimate care-taking tool? Don't only *do* things that are in your best interest, but—this is key— go out of your way to remind yourself frequently that you're proud of what you're doing or did. When you take actions that are rational and healthy, it's crucial that you don't brush them off with a, "Well, I wish I'd done this yesterday," or, a "Big deal, so I did one teensy thing that's good for me."

You might be thinking, "But, how can I be proud when I should have been doing something anyway?" Clients say this to me all the time. It's called minimizing, and it makes you feel smaller when you want to make your positive strides feel big, important, and valuable.

Minimization leads to disempowerment, which is not the direction you want to move in. Make a big deal of any actions that make you feel proud.

For example, maybe you and Ben & Jerry's spent some time together last night. Then tonight you brought home fresh salmon and put some farro in the rice cooker, made yourself a nice little salad, and had a lovely dinner by yourself (with no computer or TV as company), marveling at every delicious bite. It's crucial to mark your dinner at home in the positive column and enjoy that you gave this gift to yourself. This means allowing yourself to focus on feeling proud of your dinner at home, rather than feeling ashamed of the time you spent palling around with Ben & Jerry's.

The idea is to take your efforts seriously and recognize that, even in your funk, you can always, *always* do something to take care of yourself. When you've overeaten or watched TV instead of going for a run, you can do a load of laundry or wash the dishes that have piled up in the kitchen sink, hug your daughter and tell her she's a fantastic kid, call your father to see how he's doing though he's forgotten again that it's his turn to call you, or make a doctor's appointment you've been putting off. When you're ashamed, doing something—anything—positive to make yourself proud turns everything around and morphs a loss into a win.

Many dysregulated eaters think that when life gets better they'll have the time or energy or motivation to care well for themselves. The opposite is true. Only when you take excellent care of you will life truly improve in a deep, meaningful, sustainable way. Self-caring doesn't come from having the time or energy for it. It comes from making time or finding energy. It's a loving gift from you to you that is available for practice every hour of every day. It says I'm worth it, lovable, and valuable all the time, and I'm going to treat myself that way no matter what else is happening in my life or how others treat me.

Here are some things you can do for yourself followed by spending a minute or two glorying in being proud that you did:

- Go grocery shopping and come home with a cart full of healthy, delicious foods.
- Take a walk, hit the gym, or dance around your living room till you work up a sweat.
- Watch a short video on deep breathing and learn how to manage your breath.
- Clean one small space in your living quarters, just enough to see an improvement.
- Do one thing on your to-do list (you don't need to knock out the whole list to feel proud).
- Look at the mirror and gaze only at your best features.
- Explore volunteering or think about how to help a friend.
- Make your bed or wash the car.
- Get a head start on doing your taxes by organizing your paperwork.
- Call, text, or email a friend or family member you haven't seen or heard from in a long time.
- Water your plants.
- Clean out the cat's litter box.
- Bathe the dog.
- Get a book or sign up for a course on learning how to meditate.

The point of these acts is to get out of shame-based mental territory and stop shame-inducing behavior. It's to show yourself that you *can* get things done, that you *are* responsible, and that you *have* the power to behave in ways that make you proud—big ways, small ways, it doesn't matter. It's also to experience and become more comfortable with being proud of yourself and making it your permanent state of being. Sure, when life seems crummy, you may forget that you have the power of proud. In truth, you always have it whether you're using it or not, just as the sun is always up there in the sky even when we see nothing but clouds.

Are there other ways to help me feel proud of myself?

Here are two mental constructs I learned about in social work school and have cherished over the decades because I find them useful personally and professionally: the *observing ego* and the *ego ideal*. They constitute a paradox that enables you to stay motivated to grow and change through striving to become the person you wish to be while knowing you never will fully become that person.

The first construct is the *observing ego*, which is "that part of the self that has no effects, engages in no actions, and makes no decisions. It functions in conflict-free states to merely witness what it sees. It is like a camera that records without judgment. It is never weighing any thought, gesture or action on the scale of right and wrong, sane or insane, good or bad."[1] Of course, because it's a cognitive process, there's no actual part of the mind where this observing ego is tucked away.

I bet you've used your observing ego before and weren't aware that it had a name. Say you're waiting for a friend in a park or at a restaurant, and you're just watching what's going on. In the park, a man trips on an uneven patch of sidewalk and then walks on as if nothing happened, or you feel the breeze of a skater whizzing by on her skateboard. In the restaurant, you watch as a young child whispers in the ear of his father, and they both giggle while two tired-looking waiters chatter in Greek near the swinging door to the kitchen.

You're neither causing these behaviors nor doing anything to change them. You're simply noticing their occurrence, holding them nonjudgmentally in your awareness. Maybe when you get home later you'll tell someone about the man tripping or how the child made his father laugh, but that's later and this is now, and now involves only observing and registering—and this is key—without judgment.

Another mental construct, the *ego ideal*, is "the inner image of oneself as one wants to become."[2] It is the best self we wish we could be, never mind that we'll never get there, humans being hardwired as we are by our ancient DNA. It's our vision of who we would be if we could be—which we can't—our best version of ourselves with all the latest updates, bells, and whistles.

For example, my clinical ego ideal is to listen better than I do and interrupt my clients less, to ask more motivational interviewing questions and make fewer clinical interpretations. I'd like to think that I inch toward this ideal, but I suspect that several more lifetimes wouldn't get me there. And that's all right. I'm happy to have a shining star to guide me in a worthwhile direction.

Can you see the amazing possibilities for moving forward and feeling proud when the observing ego and the ego ideal go hand in hand? The observing ego impartially monitors what you're doing in your quest to live according to your ideal blueprint. If your ego ideal is to be kind to yourself after a whopper of a binge, your observing ego notices that you either were or weren't. It is a pure, unvarnished self-reflection that is crucial for change and the ideal meld with pride to spark ongoing motivation.

Here's how it works. Rather than prod ourselves to be as we think we should or ought to be, why not think and act in ways that will help us become who we hope and aspire to be? The function of the ego ideal is to beckon us forward to behave in ways that keep us in sync with our best intentions. Naturally, the ideal self is different for each of us. Some of us wish to be conformists, while others yearn to be trailblazers. We may desire to be creative, compassionate, selfless, tolerant, enlightened, kind, worldly, wise, accomplished, and more. Wanting to live up to these ideals keeps us striving for them, all the while recognizing that we always will be only becoming. The aim is never to be perfect; it's to keep reaching for the brass ring knowing that even if we occasionally touch it we don't get to take it home with us.

Understanding these constructs—neutral self-observation and striving for a humane personal ideal—will make it easier for you to recognize when you're proud of yourself. Keeping them in mind is a very powerful tool to maintain motivation toward "normal" eating, better health, and improved self-caring.

Got any helpful mantras?

Seeing as life doesn't always go our way, it's crucial to have a set of phrases or mantras at hand that will kick in self-soothing self-talk as soon as possible. My favorite mantras are based on truths I firmly believe. Occasionally, I'll say something else to myself to suit a particular situation, but these are my go-to self-to-self messages:

- *I'm doing the best I can.* I say this to myself often, as a quick fix to perfectionist tendencies that nudge me from time to time. Many of us keep pushing ourselves until we're hurt or exhausted, and for what? Usually to come close to or reach some abstract ideal or, more often, someone else's idea of a job well done. What if, due to inborn limitations, our best isn't going to help us achieve that ideal ever? Said another way, sometimes our best is good enough, and sometimes it isn't, but often it's as far as we can go. Reminding myself that I've done my best and can do no more makes me proud of my efforts and achievements and helps me acknowledge my limitations and let go of my imperfections.

- *This is good enough.* This phrase goes along with "I'm doing the best I can" and means that *I* get to decide what's enough, not some ideal to measure myself against or another person's vision for or of me. The phrase is infused with empowerment and generates self-confidence. It says, "I don't care what anyone else thinks about how I'm doing. I care, I'm the one who counts, and I'm satisfied." It's neither an excuse nor a way to avoid accountability. It's a factual statement that I'm in charge of how well I want to do, no matter what.

- *This too shall pass.* There's a reason this phase is so commonly heard. It exudes worldly wisdom and is a gentle reminder that life is always transforming itself and that we get to hold on to neither the parts that bring us pleasure nor those that bring us pain (except through memory, of course). Usually physical and emotional suffering pass, and that's important to remember when we're in their grip. Recalling that there were and will again be pleasurable times puts whatever pain we're going through into perspective and gives us hope for a better future. Even the pain of dying passes eventually, whether or not we've made peace with it happening.

- *I'm safe and fine.* Often we get all shook up when we're caught in the clutches of memory when a current situation is similar to a previously distressing or traumatizing one. For example, when your control-freak boss who is always on your case about deadlines reminds you of how your mom was a stickler for rules like getting your homework done before going out to hang with the gang. Or when a tipsy stranger at a party who starts pawing at you reminds you of how Uncle Charlie was a little too huggy-touchy for your twelve-year-old taste when he used to come over to visit. We all have flashback-like memories that signal danger when we're actually perfectly safe.

The key is to distinguish whether we're in recall and feeling unsafe because a distressing memory has been triggered or we're in reality and are likely safe. That is, we must understand that we're feeling heightened anxiety or upset from what happened in our memory and not from any real threat in our current situation. So when I get a twinge of uncomfortable memory, the first thing I ask myself is, "Am I safe now?" When I recognize that there's no actual emotional or physical threat, I can tell myself to relax and my pulse and breath slow down almost immediately. Assuring ourselves that we're usually safe whenever we feel emotionally threatened is powerful and useful self-talk that makes all the difference in reducing distress, especially the kind that could lead to unwanted eating.

Would you feel better as you go through life if you used the above self-talk or your own version of it? If you could awaken tomorrow morning and from then on use these positive messages and mantras, how would your life improve? Of course, you may have other phrases that would work as well or better, ones that are uplifting and affirming, speak a universal truth, lower anxiety, and make you feel empowered in a healthy way. Take some time to consider what phrases would work for you—and don't hesitate to borrow mine.

●●●

Now that you know how to change your internal monologue or dialogue, you're all set for generating healthier emotions and actions, not only around food and your body, but in all aspects of life. Remember that success around eating and self-caring has nothing to do with willpower and everything to do with brainpower, especially word power. It's time to crank up your smarts to decide and change how you're going to talk to yourself for the rest of your life. It may be the most important decision you ever make.

We all have a stream of consciousness flowing beneath the surface of awareness. Sometimes it burbles or babbles, and sometimes it pounds like the surf. It may go quiet occasionally, but often it's messing with us on a volume so low that we get the intent of the message without picking up every word.

Hopefully, after reading this book, at least you now know that you have a choice: You can either keep brainwashing yourself with talk that not only doesn't help you but deeply hurts you, or you can learn a new language, adopt a healthier vocabulary that you may never have known existed. My money's on you thinking that this would be a perfect time to do a 180 with your self-talk.

What are you thinking and saying to yourself right now as this book draws to a close? If it has made you feel positive about yourself, more empowered and hopeful about your future, and you're feeling proud that you read it, you're ready to take your new words on the road. If you're not feeling positive, now is the exact moment to stop reading and come up with self-talk that says you're worth it and insists that you can change.

Start now—not tomorrow or the next day. Say something that's empowering, hopeful, loving, challenging, inspiring, intentional, self-compassionate, self-validating, and self-loving. Say several somethings: words, phrases, sentences, it doesn't matter. If you need to reread the whole book or portions of it because these ideas haven't firmly taken root, begin again or choose a passage that lightens your heart. What you say right now and from here on in has the power to heal your eating problems and lead you into a permanent recovery that will be wondrous beyond your dreams.

●●●

Case Study: **Aldo**

Aldo, a seventy-six-year-old retired police officer, began our first session by saying that he was probably "too far gone for help" at 372 pounds—150 of it gained since he was forced to retire from the force due to a serious back injury that happened in the line of duty. Pain still plagued him, but he refused to make an appointment with an orthopedist, and his cholesterol and blood pressure were "sky high." He barely left the house, fearing that someone he knew would see him at his current size, and he refused to undress in front of or have sex with his wife who, after five decades of marriage, still thought he walked on water. She's the one who gave him the "Quit Fighting with Food" workshop flyer of mine from the local library and insisted that he call me.

Shame became a theme in our sessions. Aldo was no stranger to it. His father, a retired policeman, suffered from alcoholism and rageaholism, and his mother never protected Aldo and his siblings from his dad's physical and verbal abuse. Aldo did as he was told in order to remain well under Dad's radar. His dyslexia made school difficult, and it took him three tries (the maximum) to get into the policy academy. Moreover, from ages six to nine, Aldo was sexually abused by a neighborhood priest, a trauma he'd tried to forget. He told no one about this secret shame until his marriage, and it took many months of therapy for him to talk about it with me.

His self-talk about everything, especially weight, was self-disparaging and was meant to shame him into better behavior:

- I'm worthless and didn't amount to anything, just like my dad said would happen.
- My weight tells it like it is: I'm a big, fat nothing.
- I'm proud of my wife and the kids and grandkids; that's what I'm proud of.

- I should go to doctors, hit the gym, eat better, but what's the point?
- I'm not worth your time trying to help me, and I don't know why you bother.

I explained what trauma and abuse do to a person emotionally, including how they can create a shame-based identity. We talked about him wrongly carrying the shame for everything his parents did to him and for the priest who molested him. We discussed how insidious shame is and how we need to let go of what isn't ours in order to be healthy and keep our sanity. He didn't ask for the parents he had, dyslexia, or a back injury, or to be molested by someone he should have been able to trust implicitly. He'd had a job to be proud of and a wife and family who loved him in spite of everything he thought was wrong with him.

Changing his self-talk helped to lift the shame that had been burdening Aldo for decades. Now his job was to feel proud each day by speaking to himself positively:

- I am deserving and worthy of love, caring, and enjoying a happy life.
- I am proud of what I've survived and achieved.
- People love me, and I can love myself at my current weight.
- I will feed my body well and take better care of it.
- I will think of myself as a trauma survivor, not a victim.

In order to change his feelings about himself, particularly shameful ones, Aldo needed to understand the incorrect meaning he'd assigned to events in his life, especially in childhood. Because he attached a meaning of "shame on *me*" rather than "shame on *you*," he believed that he deserved to feel shame and spoke to himself with disgust and condemnation. His self-talk reflected back to him the evils he saw in himself. But once he recognized that he was blameless and worthy all along, he could be proud of having overcome many hurdles and begin to identify and use self-talk that reflected the light he had always carried within him.

ENDNOTES

Chapter 1

[1] Vironika Tugaleva, *The Art of Talking to Yourself: Self-Awareness Meets the Inner Conversation* (Ontario: Soulux Press, 2017), 14.

[2] Remez Sasson, "How Many Thoughts Does Your Mind Think in One Hour?," Success Consciousness, accessed 7/14/20, https://www.successconsciousness.com/blog/inner-peace/how-many-thoughts-does-your-mind-think-in-one-hour/.

Chapter 2

[1] Albert Ellis and Robert Harper, *A Guide to Rational Living* (New York: Institute for Rational Living, 1961), 91.

Chapter 3

[1] Kristin Neff, *Self-Compassion: The Proven Power of Being Kind to Yourself* (New York: HarperCollins Publishers, 2011), 10.

[2] Amy Cuddy, "Your Body Language May Shape Who You Are," filmed June 2012 in Edinburgh, Scotland, TED video, 20:48, https://www.ted.com/talks/amy_cuddy_your_body_language_shapes_who_you_are?language=en.

Chapter 4

[1] Laura Starecheski, "Why Saying Is Believing—The Science of Self-Talk," *Shots*, NPR's *Health News*, October 7, 2014, https://www.npr.org/sections/health-shots/2014/10/07/353292408/why-saying-is-believing-the-science-of-self-talk.

Chapter 6

[1] Christopher Basten and Stephen Touyz, "Sense of Self: Its Place in Personality Disturbance, Psychopathology, and Normal Experience,"

Review of General Psychology 24, no. 2 (October 2019), https://doi.org /10.1177/1089268019880884.

Chapter 8

[1] Kate Williamson, "Conducting User Interviews: Lessons Learned," Centerline Digital, November 14, 2013, https://www.centerline.net/blog /conducting-user-interviews-lessons-learned/.

[2] Salman Akhtar, *Comprehensive Dictionary of Psychoanalysis* (New York: Routledge, 2009), 89.

BIBLIOGRAPHY

Akhtar, Salman. *Comprehensive Dictionary of Psychoanalysis*. New York: Routledge, 2009.

Basten, Christopher, and Stephen Touyz. "Sense of Self: Its Place in Personality Disturbance, Psychopathology, and Normal Experience." *Review of General Psychology* 24, no. 2 (October 2019). https://doi.org /10.1177/1089268019880884.

Cuddy, Amy. "Your Body Language May Shape Who You Are." Filmed June 2012 in Edinburgh, Scotland. TED video, 20:48. https://www. ted.com/talks/amy_cuddy_your_body_language_shapes_who_you _are?language=en.

Ellis, Albert and Robert Harper. *A Guide to Rational Living*. New York: Institute for Rational Living, 1961.

Neff, Kristin. *Self-Compassion: The Proven Power of Being Kind to Yourself*. New York: HarperCollins Publishers, 2011.

Sasson, Remez. n.d. "How Many Thoughts Does Your Mind Think in One Hour?" Success Consciousness. https://www.successconsciousness.com /blog/inner-peace/how-many-thoughts-does-your-mind-think -in-one-hour/.

Starecheski, Laura. "Why Saying Is Believing—The Science of Self-Talk." *Shots*. NPR's *Health News*, October 7, 2014. https://www.npr.org /sections/health-shots/2014/10/07/353292408/why-saying-is-believing -the-science-of-self-talk.

Tugaleva, Vironika. *The Art of Talking to Yourself: Self-Awareness Meets the Inner Conversation*. Ontario: Soulux Press, 2017.

Williamson, Kate. "Conducting User Interviews: Lessons Learned." Centerline Digital, November 14, 2013. https://www.centerline.net/blog /conducting-user-interviews-lessons-learned/.

INDEX

conscious, 73–74

destructive self-talk about, 25–26

ending eating, 74–76

examples of self-talk about, 14–15

food cravings and, 71–73

food thoughts prior to, 70–71

in front of a mirror, 96

"healthy," 3

"I crave→I think→I eat or do something else," 77–78

importance of self-talk for, 12–13

journaling about, 81

mindful, 39, 51, 73–74, 75, 154

mindless, 73, 79

negative self-talk about, 25–26

post-eating check-in, 76–77

rationality used to make decisions about, 78–79

in social situations.*See* social situations

stopping, 74–76

ego ideal, 159, 160

Ellis, Albert, 36

emotions. *See also* pride; shame

choosing *vs.* avoiding, 31

destructive self-talk about your, 29

of dysregulated eaters, 41–42

food thoughts and, 70

intense, before and after eating, 79

primary, 23

secondary, 23

self-talk for managing uncomfortable, 102–104

self-validation and staying attuned to your, 57–58

smart self-talk and experiencing painful, 42

empowering self-talk, 43–44

ending eating, 74–76

exercise. *See* fitness

external motivators, 34, 37, 39, 149–150

F

failure oriented, destructive self-talk as, 16

"faking it til you make it," 64–66

family members. *See also* parents

attitudes about eating and weight, 8, 124–126

bullying about weight from, 11

dysregulated eaters eating with, 124–125

healthy *vs.* unhealthy self-talk about food and weight when with, 127–130

Fat is a Feminist Issue (Orbach), 57, xiv

fat shaming, 10–11

feelings. *See* emotions

fitness

challenging self-talk about, 46

destructive self-talk about, 29–30

empowering self-talk about, 44

hopeful self-talk about, 44–45

inspiring self-talk about, 47

intentional self-talk about, 48

loving self-talk about, 45

self-compassionate self-talk about, 53

smart self-talk for, 106–108

food

challenging self-talk about, 46

destructive self-talk about, 25–26

empowering self-talk about, 44

healthy *vs.* unhealthy self-talk with family about, 127–130

hopeful self-talk about, 44–45

inspiring self-talk about, 47

intentional self-talk about, 48

loving self-talk about, 45

rationality used to make decisions about, 78–80

self-compassionate self-talk about, 53

shortcut to discovering if you really want, 78

socializing centering around, 117

as a solution to other difficulties, 21